Heal.Thy.Man
METHOD

A Pocketbook Guide To Self-Awareness
And Fulfillment For Men

Heal.Thy.Man Method
A Pocketbook Guide To Self-Awareness And
Fulfillment For Men

Published by Creation Publishing Group LLC

www.creationpublishing.com

© 2022 Creation Publishing Group

ISBN # 979-8-9857286-0-6

Library of Congress Number # 9798985728606

Published and printed in the United States of America.

Heal.Thy.Man
M E T H O D

A Pocketbook Guide To Self-Awareness
And Fulfillment For Men

BY
Paul Randolph Newell

Table of Contents

Table of Contents

Acknowledgments

First and foremost, I want to acknowledge "The All," also known as The Divine, Source, Jehovah, Allah, Yahweh. Without this energy and presence in life, none of this is conceived and brought to manifest.

Bless up to those that came before me and laid paths in DNA and energy. Thank you for all of you.

Bless up to my Brothers that I've accumulated through The Mankind Project, Men Mentoring Men, All Kings, and The Brothahood of Kings Collective. You Men have been friends, family, support, guidance, and light when I was in darkness. I appreciate you.

Love and gratitude to and for my siblings my Brothers (Henley, Christoff, Carlyle, Wayne) and Sisters (Marjorie, Marcia, Elizabeth) in blood and family bond. Our relationships have had highs and lows, and regardless of the tide, I always know you love and care for me as I do for you.

To my next ones, Elijah, Noah, and Marley... I'm always at your side in energy and spirit and will always be here for you when you are ready. Any questions you have about me may be answered on these pages.

And lastly, I acknowledge and bless YOU, the reader, for being willing to ride the wave of self-awareness and self-fulfillment. Blessings to you.

Paul

Foreword

By Coach Michael Taylor

Now more than ever, men need resources to support them in embracing a new paradigm of masculinity. The media-generated perception is men are arrogant, violent, non-emotional, selfish, greedy, inconsiderate, and only think about sex and money. The truth is that all men are capable of being loving, sensitive, caring, vulnerable, compassionate, and empathetic.

What makes it so difficult for men to embrace these qualities is the constant barrage of negative images and stories about them that constantly fill our airwaves. We are continuously bombarded with stories of toxic masculinity (which doesn't actually exist), senseless acts of violence, domestic abuse, corporate corruption, and a myriad of other negative male stereotypes that create the perception that men are the bad guys.

The good news is that more and more men are waking up to the idea that the current paradigm of masculinity is no longer sustainable. Men are now open to a new conversation in which they embrace new ways of being and relating as men. By embracing the new and evolved roles of masculinity, men are learning how to create deeper relationships and more fulfilling careers. Instead of chasing fame, they are pursuing fulfillment which leads them to find their passions and purpose, resulting in men leading more joyful lives.

For more than 25 years, I have been writing about the changing roles of manhood and masculinity. Whenever I encounter a man helping usher in the new paradigm of masculinity I'm speaking about, it fills me with excitement and optimism about the future of men's work and how it can help eradicate a lot of the social ills that currently plague our world.

Paul Randolph Newell is a man who is on a mission to support and empower men to embrace this new paradigm of masculinity I'm speaking about. In his new book: Heal.Thy.Man, he has put together a powerful resource guide for any man who is ready to move past antiquated ways of being a man and embrace new and exciting ways in which men learn to connect with their authentic selves, allowing them to live fully authentic lives filled with passion and purpose.

This insightful guidebook serves as a roadmap for men to follow to support them in embodying healthy, authentic masculinity and creating more rewarding and fulfilling lives.

Intro

When my Mom was alive, I remember her telling me repeatedly that I should write a book.

That phrase usually came after some ordeal, or challenge, or insight that changed me in some way. After she passed, I could still hear her voice in my ears and heart telling me to write. I would write in my journals, and write poems, and such, and nothing of this level.

This book is a collection of lessons in my life that I think are worth the share to help other Men that may encounter similar circumstances.

As I'm writing this book, masculinity is being redefined, rewired, reworked. And what is all that based on?

I've become skeptical of the campaigns on masculinity because I think it is crafting a narrative of what a Man is supposed to be. Now take that, and add in the variable of being a Man of Color, or being a non-custodial Dad, or being below a socio-economic stat line, or being a masculine identifying being.

My journey over the years has been and is figuring out what it means to be a Man. Years ago when I THOUGHT I knew, my health began to deteriorate and I added health to the mix in regards to how do I take care of myself as a Man.

Welcome to Heal.Thy.Man Methods and congratulations of your investment in yourself and your alignment.

My name is Paul and I will be your Guide, Narrator, Teacher, and Support on this Journey. I laid out this journey for you because I know there is potential in you.

You may be thinking, "you have never met me", and while that may be correct, with the technologies I have learned and integrated over the past ten years, I'm confident the experience and stories in these pages will resonate with you on some level.

This book will be free of telling you what to do or how to do it. Instead, I will invite you to explore various things in yourself and your life that can be celebrated, acknowledged, reprogrammed, and aligned. Please note, throughout the book, I will refer more to myself because these are methods that I have either learned or taught myself, and I continue to use them for my sanity in my world of chaos.

And as Men, it's helpful for us to have methods to use in chaos because, personally, the teaching of managing my emotions, sensations, and feelings in times of change was non-existent. So my curious self-went seeking.

I have yet to know your story, and maybe one day I will, but until then, whatever brought you to this book means there is something in this that will be useful for you.

This book will expand on three exploratory stages of an adult Man (18 and above, and if you are younger than that and reading this, well, HOT DAMN, keep reading because you are ahead of the game. Oh, and I apologize in advance for the cursing).

The three stages are as follows:

Step Into the Arena

These guides (lessons) focus on the journey of teaching self-exploration. There will be prompts, questions, assignments, and treasure hunts (yes, treasure hunts) for you to give a go so you can learn more about yourself, and explore yourself.

Master Your Mojo

These lessons focus on how I taught myself to integrate what I've learned about myself to move through the world... authentically. In these lessons, there will be more prompts, questions, assignments, meditations, and missions.

The Rise Into Your King

These guides focus on how a Man connects with his Dharma/Purpose and creates a mission and what that can look like in the world. This can be difficult for Men because there has yet to be any curriculum out there about finding a mission.

And why is mission important?

Ayn Rand said it best, "The Man without a purpose is a Man who drifts at the mercy of random feelings or unidentified urges and capable of any evil because he is totally out of control of his own life."

Welcome to the experience, Men, and enjoy the lessons in Heal.Thy.Man Method.

Step Into The Arena

Drawing by Paul Newell

"Face the most fierce, savvy, and powerful opponent ever… yourself."

Paul Randolph Newell

What is an Arena?

An arena is a large enclosed platform, usually circular or oval-shaped, that is a showcase for sporting events, theater, and performances.

This is also a place of entertainment... to entertain the ideas and concepts of stepping into yourself and battling the image and story that you've had of yourself for the majority, if not all of your life. Once you've exposed yourself to yourself and come to the edge with the parts of yourself that you've denied, or suppressed, then, and only then, can you truly begin to master yourself and shift your environment.

When I chose to step into the arena, I knew it was a threshold for me and a place that only I could go. As much as I had learned over time, I had internal blocks that I avoided, which prevented me from integrating what I learned.

For me, the term "stepping into the arena" put some depth into the process of going inside and battling my greatest opponent... myself.

So what is the purpose of stepping into an arena in regards to self awareness and well-being? This is the place to put your past performances, events, and battles on showcase. Put them out there for you to see, and then battle.

To give another perspective on the opportunity of stepping into the arena to face self, I'm sharing terms and concepts that align with me and may align with you too. As you read on, jot down notes, feelings, and impressions, and in this guide, use whatever space you'd like to add in your thoughts and comments.

To heal myself, I realized it was time to step into the arena of myself to determine what I get to address to thrive in my circumstances. For years, I blamed others, became a victim of my situations and circumstances, and reveled in the mishaps I perceived in my lifetime to date.

"If this person had done (insert action)."

"If the system wasn't so messed up, I would be able to (insert desire/want)."

Have you ever started sentences this way? And if you have, I think this section will resonate with you, and if those phrases are foreign to you, this is still for you too and confirms for me that you're in the right place.

Those phrases are phrases of the victim. The victim gets thrown into an Arena most likely to die or to be a source of entertainment because the spectators fail to take the victim seriously.

In this instance, I go into the Arena knowing I'll win and ready to experience the lessons and journey to my victory. This section is an opportunity to see yourself in a way that will support your growth, self-awareness, and ascension.

The space for reflection in this portion of the method will provide insight on the stories you tell yourself about love, life, loss, the patterns that govern your life, acknowledgment of the ways you guard yourself as well as uncover the source of your actions and pillars of your support.

My invitation to you is to approach this section free of judgment of yourself, free of judgment of your situation, and free of judgment of your experiences. This is a space to be a spectator of the events in your life that will come up as you battle the parts of yourself that are conditioned, stuck, or disconnected. Let's step in.

"We are the stories we tell ourselves."

Joan Didion

What's My Story

So, what's your story?

Depending on the tone of the voice that speaks those words, they can take on different intentions. When it comes down to aligning the body, mind, and soul, I ask myself that question with a curious tone.

I can remember when I participated in personal development training in North Carolina, and there was a phrase that would get thrown around, and it was, "you're in story." At first, that shit used to piss me off when someone said that to me.

In my head, I would say, "These people don't know me." Then, one day in training, I took that phrase a little further and said, "These people don't know me; they don't know my STORY!"

And BOOM, it hit me; I WAS in story. I was in a narrative that shaped my reality. I was in a boxed perception of life, love, and loss. As I write this, I am experiencing the sunken feeling I had at that moment. Acknowledging that I was living a story, with the combination of me loving to beat myself up, I found myself reflecting on how my stories impacted me and others in my life.

I was in that sunken place for a couple of weeks and then slowly (slowly meaning years) began revising my story.

When I confronted my stories, my perceptions began to change.

When tough situations arose, I reverted to a story, and shifting my story seemed like magic because my situations could change almost immediately. Then in other moments, it seemed like an insurmountable task to shift my story because I wanted to keep my story for fear that I may not know who I am without it.

So here's how the story changed; I asked myself the following things, and I invite you to do the same.

What is the story I have about my life?

What is the story I have about love in my life?

What is the story I have about the loss in my life?

I tend to take myself too seriously, so I have to make this fun and play it up like a short story or short film on Netflix. This allowed me to take myself out of my situation and explore myself as if I was engaged in the backstory of the character development of a television program or novel.

When stepping into my Arena to address my stories, this is getting to the roots of the subtle and influential conditioning I have grown in. Please be aware that this is a practice of exploration and revision. In the Arena, we battle and break down the stories we have been living in and be free of judgment.

My Story About Life...

"Life is hard. I grew up in a household of divorce; my mom and dad split when I was four or five, and we lived in an affluent, predominantly white town. I always felt different and sensed I was different, although I had yet to know how as a young kid. I was always encouraged to be humble regardless of my accomplishments.

I grew up seeing my mom clean houses for affluent white people and get paid and gifts to help with her kids. I grew up seeing my dad have his own Taxi service, and now looking back, I wonder how he stayed afloat or what his days looked like. I remember my mom stressing over money and getting the impression that nothing was easy to come by. I have to work hard for everything I get, and sometimes I work two to five times harder than anyone else.

Growing up, I was teased and unaccepted by some white kids and rejected by most black kids because I wasn't "black enough." So I isolated, kept to myself, and began wearing masks and people-pleasing to be accepted.

As I got older, I kept wearing the mask because I realized there are dangers of being a Man in the skin that I'm in. Because of that, I chose to pass on many opportunities. I chose to cover and hide myself and my feelings. Rather than stand out as the lead, I chose to play a role."

SUMMARY: To get through life, I thought I had to be someone other than myself.

Was there a part of this story that resonated with you? If so, which part?

What emotions/thoughts came up for you?

Did my story bring up something in you? Did it bring up a part of your story?

My Story About Love…

"I have no idea what love is, and I'm difficult to love. My parents divorced, my dad was abusive, my mom was in survival mode, and loving energy was felt in the form of provision rather than adoration.

Before I got married and divorced, I kept multiple sexual partners to feel fully received and avoid abandonment. My thinking was that I'd rather hurt them before they hurt me. I thought that love was just like in the movies and that people loved each other unconditionally, but my love life experiences have shown me otherwise. In most of my past relationships, I've had relationships on the side. A woman on the side to have sex with or, in most cases, get a blowjob and that would satisfy and express a part of myself I was unable to express in my main relationship.

I've always thought that if I show all of myself to one person, they could never love me, so I cemented that story by thinking I need multiple partners to feel fulfilled and whole. I thought that love was dangerous and sneaky and would end up hurting me in the long run, so I looked for any crack in my relationship foundation to support my story that my partner will leave."

SUMMARY: Love is a lie, and no one will ever love me as Me.

Was there a part of this story that resonated with you? If so, which part?

What emotions/thoughts came up for you?

Did my story bring up something in you? Did it bring up a part of your story?

My Story About Loss...

"My first experience with loss came at seven years old when Mr. Macey died. Mr. Macey was an older man that lived next door to the house my whole family lived in before my parents separated. He was 'Big Paul,' and I was 'Lil Paul,' and I was with him whenever I could get the chance. I knew and felt that he cared for me. When he passed, I was devastated until I saw his body in a casket. At that moment, I recognized that he had left his body, and all that was left was a shell. I also recognized at that moment I grieved losing my time with him, losing the care I felt from him, and losing my friend.

Several years later, my best friends Richie and Gregory moved to Florida, and I recalled that my bike also got stolen during that time. My mom tried comforting me when my bike got stolen; I told her, 'I feel like a bird without wings,' and I remember saying that like it was yesterday.

At that time in my life, I hardened my heart and protected it because I never wanted to feel that pain, that hurt again. I knew at a young age that life would bring loss, and my remedy to address it is to stay detached and never fully give all of myself to anyone or anything because WHEN I lose them, I'll be okay instead of devastated."

SUMMARY: Never commit to anything because you will lose it.

Was there a part of this story that resonated with you? If so, which part?

What emotions/thoughts came up for you?

Did my story bring up something in you? Did it bring up a part of your story?

Your story may be longer or shorter, more in-depth, or less in-depth; either way, it's YOUR story. It's a narrative that you are aligned to, for now, and it brings with it its own set of conditions, actions, and language that will keep you in that story.

So now what?

Look at your stories on Life, Love, and Loss. Those three areas span across many other areas in life and how we respond to them.

Before moving on, look at your stories from a hawk's eye perspective. A hawk can see the big picture and the small details. Pay close attention to all the messages from what you observe. Tap into your intuition and keep your eyes, ears, mind, and heart open.

You're observing this piece of work and determining if it resonates with you? Acknowledge the benefits, the impact, and the outcomes. If it resonates, keep your story. If it fails to resonate or bring about a sense of calm, ease, and bliss, it gets to be revised so it resonates and aligns with you.

My stories failed to serve me, and it became time to revise, rewrite, and rewire to create something new in my life. The next step was to take another scoop into my stories to acknowledge the patterns I have created in my life to keep these stories front and center.

In this process, I recognized my stories created patterns of how I moved through life.

My patterns and habits create my results...

Paul R. Newell

Your Patterns Tell A Tale

Within my stories, I became aware of the moves and tactics I would take when I was in my story. I identify them as my patterns, my go-to's to numb myself to validate my stories. I committed to myself that it was necessary to adjust my patterns to move forward differently.

So what are patterns?

By definition, a pattern is a model or design used as a guide. As a verb, it means to give a regular or intelligible form to something. Patterns are developed at an early stage in all of our lives. We do something, we get something, we do that thing again, we get more of something, and before you know it, a pattern has developed.

After bringing awareness to my story, then started re-writing it, I recognized my pull to certain situations. To be specific, these "certain situations" are really chaos.

I LOVE THE CHAOS!!! Yep, I said it. I love the chaos, and THAT realization helped me discover my patterns.

I took a hard look at my past relationships and their ends, all of my past jobs and how they ended, how I dealt with responsibilities, and how I dealt with suc-cess, and all came back to a set pattern that I adopted to keep me "safe."

In this case, "safe" means protected from criticism, re-jection, and on a deeper level, protected from love, sup-port, fulfillment, and grace.

When I've discussed this concept of patterns with past clients and in Men's circles, "Patterns" quickly become

"Habits." Please note there is a distinction between the two.

Patterns = Unconsciousness / Habits = Consciousness.

Here's an example of a **Pattern** - - if I drive the same way every day to and from work, I've established a pattern. I could go on autopilot and go that same path every time, and it's second nature.

Here's an example of **Habit** - - if I stop at Wendy's or the Gym every day as I'm coming home from work, this is a habit. I consciously choose to go to either one of those places; I could always do something different.

Still unclear? Here's another example.

Pattern - - every time I start to really love someone and feel they love me, I begin to create chaos and disconnection to sabotage the relationship and avoid any potential pain or abandonment.

Habit - - every time I start to really love someone and feel they love me, I start watching more porn and staying out late.

The pattern is that when I get a glimmer of authentic love, my unconscious uses insidious tactics to spoil the relationship. My habits are conscious choices that I employ to avoid my feelings in the space of authentic love. I could do other things like go for a hike, go to a movie, or even meditate. In this case, the habit is a product of my pattern of sabotaging my relationship and emotionally detaching to avoid rejection, abandonment, or disappointment.

When tapping into awareness of your patterns, it's important to continue as an observer of your past. This topic is another key to Stepping Into The Arena to battle self because if you are to defeat any opponent, a key piece is knowing your opponent's patterns. What are their go-tos when things get dire?

We are, by nature, creators of patterns and habits. Humans want efficiency, efficacy, and familiarity. The more we make a pattern, the stronger the pattern becomes. From a scientific perspective, when we as humans perform a pattern, a neural pathway is created. When a pattern is repeated, that pathway gets stronger.

So everyone has a pattern they revert to in various life situations.

What are yours?

To help dive into this and unearth your patterns, let's consider the results you are getting in your life.

Are you in a fulfilling relationship?

Are you in a fulfilling career?

Do your actions match your words?

Do you feel confident and worthy of having what you want?

If you answered no to any or all of these, what you're experiencing are your results. Your results are the result of your unconscious and conscious choices. The lack of fulfillment results from something thriving in you that will keep you in a pattern of dis-ease, despair, and disappointment.

Let's pause and introduce the Hermetic Principle of Causality, also known as Cause and Effect. This law of Cause and Effect states:

Causality (also referred to as causation or cause and effect) is influence by which **one event, process, state, or object (a cause) contributes to the production of** *another event, process, state, or object (an effect) where the cause is partly responsible for the effect, and the effect is partly dependent on the cause.*

"Every Cause has its Effect; every Effect has its Cause; everything happens according to Law; Chance is but a

name for Law not recognized: there are many planes of causation, but nothing escapes the Law." – The Kybalion

So if our patterns are effects, what are the causes? What, in your stories concerning love, life, and loss, have created patterns in your life that are producing your results?

This is an opportune time to go back to your recollection of your stories of Life, Love, and Loss.

As you read your stories, take moments to recall your stories and begin to get curious about an event, process, state, or object that could cause the results you are getting.

Below are prompts I used to get to the cause of my patterns. I've filled in my responses to help you understand how this process can work. Remember, embrace, and observe from a hawk eye perspective and be curious rather than judgmental and demanding.

- What is the result in my Life that I want to improve? *My relationship with my kids.*

- How long has this been a concern? *For ten years and compounding over the past nine.*

- Have you been in situations like this in the past, and if yes, when? *No and yes. This Father thing is new to me, and I resist asking for advice because most will fail to empathize with my situation of having three kids with three different women, with two of them moving to different parts of the country.*

- What is a pattern or belief you observe of yourself in these situations? *There is a pattern to armor up and play the victim to avoid giving all my Love and getting hurt and abandoned at some point. I believe I'm too fragile to handle rejection and conflict, so I people-please, avoid my boundaries, and make myself docile.*

- When you look back at your story about Love, Life, and Loss, what is a theme in your story that may be the cause of your results? *They all leave, and it's my fault.*

- Ouch...» **they all leave, and it's my fault."** As I followed the thread on that story/belief about myself, I found that the thread went all the way back to my four-year-old little self, catching the vibration of conflict and chaos bouncing off the walls in that house I lived in for the first five years of my life.

The story I started developing when I left one home and moved into another one was reinforced over years of hearing yelling, years of seeing depression, years of losing the elders that cared for me, years of me feeling alone and that no one sees me or even cares.

Acknowledging this belief in my story brought clarity to my patterns and actions regarding aspects of my Life, Love, and Loss.

Acknowledging all of this also sheds light on the patterns I employ when I'm in fear and have yet to fully trust a space. Those patterns show up in the form of armor. I notice that I defend and deflect to keep myself safe and out of harm's way.

The only problem is that the hiding steered me directly into harm's way.

Before moving on, are you willing to acknowledge your patterns? Are you willing to acknowledge the patterns that have steered you into harm's way and into prosperity's way?

Take a moment and embrace and honor the patterns that have brought you to this place in your life right now.

"if you wear a mask long enough, you forget who you are beneath it." –

Alan Moore

Armor Up

Stepping into the Arena of Self is looking at self and acknowledging the tools I employ to navigate Life, Love, and Loss. My default tool is my armor. When shit starts going left or I sense discomfort or uncertainty, I armor up.

Here is the interesting part of this in relation to stepping into the arena of self. Competitors in arena battles will most likely have a weapon and armor. I'll address the weapon in another guide; for now, let's address ARMOR.

ARMOR is a covering worn to protect the body in battle.

To ARMOR is to provide someone or something with emotional, social, or other defenses.

At first, this armor concept was foreign to me because I thought I was being open and really being selective. I became calculated in what I presented to others because I had never "felt" safe from a young age, especially when one of my early caretakers, Mr. Macey, passed. He was the first person I truly felt love from. When I close my eyes and think of my time with him, I can still feel vibrations of stability moving up and down my spine.

After he passed, I realize now I never fully trusted anyone. I started playing a role from a young age so I could be accepted or so I could fly under the radar. Those tendencies move through many areas of my life. From the type of car I drive and the color (I stay away from flashy vehicles so I can reduce my chances of getting pulled over as a Man with dark skin).

I started wearing masks to hide whatever I was feeling inside, being funny when I needed to be, quiet when I needed to be, and supportive when I needed to be. It was a curse at times and a gift in becoming skilled at reading people and energies. Scouting them out and figuring them out was guidance in who I needed to begin a given moment in different crowds.

I was focused on others to figure out how I survived in my environment. That may read heavy, and it is. When I followed the thread on my reasons for my actions of wearing a mask, it came to, I want to survive (this will be explored in another guide).

Over time, those masks created my armor because I was never connecting to my Self, so my Self armored up to protect itself... from me. I was putting in the effort to be authentic to others, and I was failing to put effort into being authentic to self. I was creating and stirring up anger and resentment, and it was slowly killing me. It all came to a head, and the best way I can explain it is through a story.

The Journey to My Heart

The journey began when I was staffing a Men's initiation weekend in the woods in NY. I have been staffing initiation weekends for seven years, yet this was the first time I was on a weekend and was free of any pain in my hips. The year prior, I had bilateral hip replacement surgery, and every experience over that year was a new experience.

On this weekend, there were various processes to support Men in getting to their wisdom and truth. One of the processes supported me in accessing and moving through my anger; and I have a lot of anger.

My activity involved using a stone and earth to express anger, and I picked up that stone and drove it into the Earth (thank you, Mama Earth, for taking my anger and transmuting it). And every time I drove the stone into the Earth, my voice got louder, and I called out the names of my kid's mothers and then claimed, you will never keep me away from them." As the last word left my mouth, I could hear and see my words moving through the trees and into the skies; then, my headache started.

After the retreat was complete, I woke up on Monday morning with a pounding headache. I felt nauseous and very anxious. When I took my blood pressure, it was 187/138, which was my green light to get my ass to the hospital.

When I got to the ER, they got me in a room and worked for hours to get my blood pressure down, with no success, so they admitted me so I could stay the night. While the doctor and nurses worked on me, I could sense their bewilderment about why I was there.

***For full transparency, my getting there was a culmination of things. First, I stopped taking my meds before the *weekend, it was hot and I drank more coffee than water, there was a lot of energy moving through the weekend, AND I was on the verge of a breakup with my Girlfriend at the time.*

As I lay in the hospital bed listening to a zen music station on the hospital tv, I started to ask myself, "Why am I here *really*?" As I asked the question, there was a flash of a voice saying, "Talk to your heart." Fortunately, I was used to doing visualization meditations, going on Shaman journeys, and creating space for that to happen. To add to this, I learned about the Omega Point Program and Parts work.

Dr. Arielle Schwartz describes parts work in this way:

"*Within parts work therapy,* **you achieve trauma resolution by recognizing disowned parts and giving these parts a voice**. *The goal is to help you develop an embodied sense of self that can compassionately hold your emotions, vulnerable sensations, and young parts of self.*"

So I started breathing, then envisioning I was at a castle and I walked in, and there was a long table in there. As I sat down on one end, my heart sat down on the other.

I say, "Heart, what's wrong? Why are you running so hot? I want us to live."

My Heart replied, "You're holding me too tight! Why are you holding me so tight?"

I start to cry.

Incessantly, my heart kept asking me, "WHY ARE YOU HOLDING ME SO TIGHT?!

And after a long pause, I couldn't take it anymore and yelled back, "I'M SICK OF THEM HURTING YOU!!! I'm sick of them cutting you, leaving you, and not giving a shit."

My heart replied, "See, you hold me tight because you protect me, and every time you get angry, you squeeze me harder. And this armor you have is rusted inside, and it's cutting me deeper."

As I calmed down, I surrendered to my heart's words and grace.

"You armored up to help me heal, and I never heal; you've been guarding us since your parents separated, over your losses, your relationships, you've been loving from anger."

I said, "I thought I was protecting you." And to that, my heart replied, "No, you've been holding us back."

I then asked my heart, "So heart, what do I do?

I could sense energy from my heart caressing my face and saying, "Set us free."

At that moment in my Shaman journey, my Ancestors came through, and they laid their burdens and pains down on the table and invited me to lay down mine. They invited me to lay down these burdens to heal and move through my pains and complete my traumas.

I was grateful to my Heart for showing me the way forward and expressing the conditions it was in. And, for bestowing upon me the title of The Heart Knight. My Heart and my Ancestors supported me in rewiring my Armor with different intentions and materials.

******

This experience was the first time I fully understood the impact of the armor I wear. The armor I was wearing looked and seemed impenetrable, yet on the inside, it was rusty and ripping me to shreds. That rust inside resulted from the internal tears and hurts I experienced over the years and was unable to express or validate.

Unfortunately, armor is something I judge all Men are conditioned to wear; then we get to spend years removing it from what's being protected.

The age-old phrases of "boys don't cry," "don't be soft," or "don't be a toxic Man" all support an internal call for Men to protect and defend. That can look like shutting down, hiding, lack of communication, and even sexual dysfunction. Every Man gets to acknowledge their armor from a neutral place, ask some questions, then be with what downloads to you.

Take moments to reflect on the ways you've armored up in your experiences with Life, Love, and Loss. If you are to take a neutral view, what was the intention for Armoring Up? Who taught you that tactic?

For me, it was to keep me safe, to protect me. Little did I know I was protecting me from me. Looking back on my experiences, I acknowledge my patterns when I employ my armor and then begin to get curious about why I really need the armor. It came down to support. I wanted to feel supported and protected, and because I perceived I was failing to get that at home, I would unconsciously figure things out on my own.

So the question is, what situations/scenarios/experiences have you Armored Up?

Here are several questions I ponder regarding my armor. I invite you to explore if you have armor. If so, ponder these questions with me:

- **What does your armor look like?**
  - ○ My armor is light green on the outside, and with my upgrades from my journey to my heart, my armor is made up of vibranium nanotech, so it's light, responsive, and molds to my skin.

- **What does your armor protect?**
  - ○ My armor protects my heart and my feelings.

- **What are the ways your armor harms you?**
  - ○ My armor blocks my heart from opening and from receiving gifts of abundance, love, and longevity.

"When we heal ourselves, we heal the past, the present, and the future."

Steven D. Farmer

Back to the Future

My stories, my patterns, and my armor all have a source of energy. Or better yet, they all have a genesis, a place where they were born into existence.

This component of stepping into my arena of self is a foundation for change. For any change or shift I want to make in my life, I get to explore the sources of my actions and patterns in the first place. Once that's been identified, I can begin discerning what support I want as I shift and what that support looks like.

This phase of the journey came when I did the Omega Point Program (O.P.P.), and I got to acknowledge and hear parts of myself and be able to peek behind the veil as to what started these trends and beliefs that appeared in my life at those moments when I took the program. I began to understand why I do the things I do, and the program gave me tools to get curious about the roots, the genesis of my pains and dis-ease.

In the program, there are inductions to bring me to a sacred space. Once there, I'm guided to different experiences to check in with different parts of self. In one instance, I was guided through a child rescue.

Before I go into this child rescue, let's review the context of this experience.

For years, I have gone on Shaman journeys and guided meditations to go back to childhood to complete traumas. For some reason or another, it was challenging for me to recall my memories before my sixth birthday. And while I knew that events had taken place, the recall was non-existent and frustrating.

The child rescue visualization in the O.P.P. was an opportunity to follow the thread to several of the beliefs

I've had about myself. Specifically, the need to be heard, the want to be seen, and the need to help others.

In this child rescue, I got to go back to a moment when I was in my crib wailing, crying hard because I wanted to get my parents' attention. My dad was beating my mom, and my mom was screaming and crying in pain. The visualization was so real that I could feel the loud voices and sounds vibrating in my eardrums, and I could hear my dad's hand hitting my mom's flesh.

And at that moment, I recognized what was happening in that version of myself that was probably about 15 or 16 months old. I could sense what I wanted and why I was crying, and it was like I was crying at the violence of everything and the fact that I couldn't do anything. In the visualization, I could sense my frustration that they didn't pay attention to me at all.

Now the key piece here is that this was the source of some of my beliefs later in life. This was the genesis of these thoughts that I've had about myself, how I show up, how I help others, and how I'm of service to others.

Now looking at this instance from a neutral point of view, I took on something far from mine; I created a story that no one saw me, no one cared, and I was insignificant to the people who were supposed to love me. My soul wanted them to see me, and my soul wanted to support and help my mother and stop my father from doing what he was doing. I was also looking to help my father and address the pain I sensed in him while he was beating my mom. Now, this is the source. Period. Now let's look at the support.

In a child rescue, I also became aware of a support system I've been told I have, yet up until that point, I failed to connect to tap into. And to be clear, this source that I connected with is the original source for everyone.

In my judgment, part of the child rescue process was to have me, as an adult, rescue me as a child. I was guided to go back to an early part of my childhood and rescue that part of myself, which has proven to be one of the most potent experiences in my life to date.

Why is that? That visualization and child rescue awakened and activated something in me to finally realize that:

I have everything I need.

I have a purpose inside of me.

I have the strength to rescue myself.

I have the wisdom of things unseen.

In my experiences to date, doing my own development/inner work and supporting other Men on their ascension, I realize that conditioning and programming can create a disconnection of who and what I am, then influence how I show up in my life.

First, consider the concept of conditioning, the circumstances affecting how people live or work, especially regarding their safety and well-being. When you were born, you were a blank slate. And yes, I know a baby is a bundle of DNA strands, and at that early stage, those strands have yet to be activated. From the time we are born until the age of seven, we grow from our conditions. This phase of our life is when we are CONDITIONED to beliefs and experiences of what safety is, stability is, as well as protection and provision.

Recalling the child rescue experience, I was conditioned in an unstable environment. In that early phase of life, I perceived my experience as unsafe because no one was paying attention to me, and people were hurting each other. So growing up in those conditions began creating my life story.

This also began creating my love story. What is love to a young one when they see pain and violence between people that brought them into the world?

From this place, let's talk about programming. Programming is input, instructions for a person or thing to behave in a predetermined way. In this case, programming is my support of the conditions I was raised in, and here's why:

> *When a being or thing is created under a condition, they are aligned to receive specific messages, do certain actions, and behave in certain ways.*

> *In that case, that being or thing becomes a frequency and will gravitate to programming that aligns with the conditions they are created/raised in.*

Men, once you have the conditions that created your stories, patterns, and armor, you can now begin to reprogram yourself by creating a support system that's conducive to who you are, what you want, and where you authentically want to go.

SUPPORT

Some may read the above and think, "Do I have a choice if I gravitate to programming that is based on how I grew up?"

And the answer is "YES!" There is always a choice, and choice begins with awareness.

Awareness regarding support is key because the people/places/things that support you may not be supporting you at all.

If you are in a place where you feel stuck, lethargic, or unmotivated, look at your support system. Is your support system the same people you've had in your life for years? Do you avoid connecting with new resources and connections? Are you comfortable asking your support for support?

What do you feel as you read those questions and think about your support? If you feel uneasy, your support system may need a change.

To give an idea of what support can be, it can be Family, Friends, Partners, your career/vocation, or your education. If any or all of those are stagnant, you will be stagnant, Men. I say stagnant because your support system is a reflection of your programming.

This results in family discord, divorces, terminations and retirement, and becoming dumb and docile.

To give you an example, I love my siblings. And over the years of my life, they have been outstanding support for me in navigating jobs, relationships, finances, and accommodations. As I got older and started to realize my conditioning, I started to experience dissonance from them. I began seeing them as people rather than my siblings, and that meant we could disagree rather than me going with everything they said while not saying anything at all or being a stand for myself.

I started to understand that my siblings were a connection to the conditions I grew up in. While they experience the same conditions differently than I do, how they navigate life, love, and loss is a reflection of how we all grew up.

For me to shift and begin creating a life that's mine, I began searching inside for what a supportive environment can be for me that will support new programming.

For me, that supportive environment is authentic, nurturing, stern and discerning, educational, curious, and fun.

Once I could identify that, my frequency shifted, I began moving toward the people/places/things aligned to who I'm becoming. Is this easy? NOPE, and it's damn sure worth it.

If you want to embark on this journey of alignment, continue onto the next section address to prepare yourself for a rebirth, and you will be creating and giving birth to a different version of yourself.

Master Your Mojo

Drawing by Paul Newell

While Mojo suggests any art that invokes supernatural powers, for us creators Mojovation means finding magic in what we do. – Robert Genn

What is Mojo? By definition, it's a magic charm, a talisman, or a spell. As an example, think of a person in your life that has an aura about them, that "IT" factor that when in their presence magical things seem to happen.

What are the qualities that come to mind about that person?

I find that as I go through my evolution and development, there are men that I go to for guidance and that I look to as role models, mentors who have a mysterious side to them. And the mystery, in my judgment, is because they've got MOJO. It's like what they set out to do is driven by something grander than themselves. I find that as I'm around them, I see magical things begin to happen.

For most of my life, I thought those Men were "just different," as if there was no way I was getting to their status or could carry that vibe.

All the most interesting things I found working with those Men is that they all were creators somehow. Once I realized that, I understood that being a creator takes bravery, patience, and resourcefulness. Over the years, I've taught myself that to tap into those characteristics of a creator, I get to practice them. Or better yet, create a practice that is fuel for one or all of these traits.

Whenever I talk about this, I think about the years of playing saxophone. The years of lessons, practice, concerts, all those goody goods were ways and spaces for me to tap into the creative part of myself. Also when I was younger, I drew often, since my younger days around seven years old. And that space has been relevant and enlightening to explore myself and what's going on inside.

In those spaces of creation and exploration, bravery can look like authentic expression. Back then, it was playing in a certain way that was distinct as me. I also drew in a fashion that people knew the art they saw was mine.

Patience can look like the many hours of practice playing scales or sections of a musical composition. And it was the same when I drew, hours on end practicing drawing faces, features, contours and all things similar. All the time practicing patience to be able to connect authentically to a part, or parts of myself and express them.

The resourcefulness is using what I am and what I got, and what I can do to create something new, something real, or something visionary.

Acknowledging mojo is an area of opportunity for Men to grow in and connect with. There is an opportunity to create something other than physical life. This has been an opportunity to truly embrace how I show up as an Authentic Man. And within that, was a path to connect with and understand feminine energy.

Connection with feminine energy supported me diving deeper into what authenticity is for me.

In 2016-17, I started deeper discovery into this "feminine thing". I put that in quotes because at the time, I considered anything with the tag "feminine" to be solely for Women, and I soon learned it was more than that.

My opening to deeper understanding of feminine energy came when I enrolled in a Shaman Training Group. This group was predominantly Women and as time went on, it was all Women and me. Over time we all got to know each other and care for each other, then became mirrors for each other in what we were going through in life at that time.

In one of our lessons, the group Leader, Eileen, explored masculine and feminine energy. She explained that everything has these energies and each being has masculine and feminine properties. Here are some of the properties I heard and retained from that lesson.

Masculine	Feminine
- Order	– Creation
- Direction	– Chaos
- Action	– Vision
- Strategy	– Nurturing
- Boundary	– Space

For years after that lesson, I explored the masculine and feminine properties in almost everything. I identified what was what in my life. For example, I identified my body as feminine, in that it creates, and is space for my mind and spirit, also as something that can be nurtured to flourish. I also identified it as masculine in that it can be in action, and be a boundary between another person or thing. This exploration was supportive in helping me unearth the masculine and feminine properties in ways to show up as a non-custodial, divorced Father.

The concept heightened when my Friend and Mentor at the time, Ivey, introduced me to the Hermetic Principles. Within them is the principle of Gender, which is what Eileen spoke of and taught me years before. The new crease in all this was "Mental Gender". The Hermetic Principles (also labeled as the Kyballion explains it best as it reads:

"The masculine principle of mind corresponds to so-called objective mind, conscious mind, voluntary mind, active mind, and the feminine principle of mind corresponds to so-called subjective mind, subconscious mind, involuntary mind, passive mind."

Dual mind, dual energies in one body. As a Man, I got curious as to what are the ways to harness this. It became clear to me it was through energy work and what that even means for me. It started with what energies do I want to explore. It was nurturing, creativity, discipline, patience, and resourcefulness.

I started challenging myself to tap into these parts and attributes within myself. Connecting to those attributes connected me to my senses and brought new life to me experiences.

My inner work and development sparked a theory on the root of Men disconnecting from their mojo, creativity and connecting to senses, and it was based on the underdevelopment of a primal energy center.... The Sacral Chakra.

Allow me to take a moment to briefly explain energy centers and the sacral chakra.

Energy centers (also known as chakras) exist throughout all living things. They provide alignment to different information and/or intentions, and relate to specific glands, hormones, and parts of our body.

I bring up energy centers in this section because this is part of your Mojo Men, and connecting with these energy centers will bring mystery to your life, and equip you to fulfill your desires and wants.

The energy center that contributes to our Mojo and creativity is the sacral energy center. Here is additional information about the Sacral Energy Center.

Purpose: Move, Connect, Feel, Have Pleasure

Element: Water

Color: Orange

When balanced a Man is: Emotionally intelligent, able to experience pleasure, can nurture self and create healthy boundaries.

When out of a balance a Man is: Emotionally manipulative, fears change, lacks desire, rigid and stiff in lower back and hips.

Connecting to this energy center opened things up for me, my creativity, and my sexual/sensual embodiment. The benefits of this connection were confirmed when I led a group of Men through a group training I named, "Dick Discipline". I experienced the magic that happens when a man learns to tap into a creative part of self. And I want to reflect on the creative part of self and what it means, or what it can mean to be a creator from that masculine / male perspective.

<u>The Dick Discipline Experience</u>

I made a commitment to a Men's group I'm in that I would complete this book in 2021. That year came and went and no book was made. I started and failed to finish. I felt like shit about it too, and I can vividly remember that feeling of thinking that I let myself down. Usually I feel bad about letting others down and could care less about me and this time was different.

As 2021 was coming to a close, I made a re-commitment to myself that this book would get done and I began thinking on what could be a spark to get this done, and then I remembered a part of a book named, "Think and Grow Rich" by Napoleon Hill, that spoke of a powerful and potent energy that can heighten imagination, willpower, and creative ability.

That energy is SEX ENERGY.

So I crafted a plan to harness my sexual energy by using breath techniques, mindfulness, visualization, masturbation techniques, semen retention strategies, and energy healing. This was more than retaining semen though. This was an experience to explore the potency of my sex and creative energies to birth this book.

Over twelve weeks me and a group of Men met every week, had homework ranging from practicing how we breath, to how we move energy in our body, to how we touch ourselves, to using our senses to manifest a vision.

I'll share more of the concepts we worked with later in this section. The Dick Discipline Experience assisted me in connecting to that part of me that is a Mystical Creator. And as I went through this, I had no idea the lessons that I would take from this; the various ways I would finally see myself and my pains, and how there were creating my world regardless of how much "inner work" I was doing.

I had to step into the arena of my darkness. And you may think that is a bad thing, and for me it was stepping into the gift of my womb, a vast, fertile space where my unconscious thoughts and beliefs thrive. This is where that Mystical Creator came in because I began to intentionally create something in my life.

A Creator can see things, people, energies, and realms. What I appreciate about creating is the allure in the balance between things that are seen and unseen. A Being that has the ability to conjure up something out of thin air, and it comes from an understanding of realms and perceptions.

That's the mojo because once that comes online, now the magic is really settling into self, accepting self for all that Self is. What I do, what I can do, and how I can show up and then begin moving in that way, performing actions that align to that mystic within me… the one within you that can create something out of nothing.

We can get lulled to sleep when we get in a pattern. We can get into a cycle of waking up, going to work, coming home, consuming an alcoholic beverage, watching television programming, maybe getting some booty now and then, and then going to bed. Repeat the pattern daily. That model is programmed into our collective environment as to our role in society.

Men, I invite you to reconnect with your mojo. To do this, you get to explore unknowns, rewire lifelines, and have great intentionality to bring forth the life that is authentic and aligned to you and only you.

Be open to the blessing...Know Your Worth...
Take Off Your Blinders
Paul R. Newell

Acknowledge & Bless

In my judgment one of the most difficult things I can do is keep an objective and positive mindset when things are going wrong. When things are falling apart, and fail to go as I wanted or expected, I tend to beat myself to a pulp, and say all sorts of bad things to myself. The words I speak to myself eventually leads to a spiral of negative and destructive thoughts and memories.

Have you ever experienced a destructive spiral? What are the ways you acknowledge and bless yourself in those self destructive spirals?

In those spirals I recall all my poor decisions and short-comings, so part of the process to master my mojo is to practice acknowledging and blessing myself. The spiral activates a victim mentally and I begin thinking, "why is this happening to me", then easily flow into a perpetrator mentally and explores the thoughts that sound like "I'll make them pay for making me feel the way I feel". It's a wild cycle and for me it's emotionally and mentally damaging. Plus it sucks my financial resources and drains my physical and mental health because the spirals lead to binges of fast food, alcohol, and over consumption of weed.

And the truth is, that dark cloud is a blessing, those incidents that I've had have been blessings because as I really settle into moving with ego and with out ego, I notice that when I acknowledge all these things that are in my life that bring me to the space that I am in right now, it's a blessing. When I choose to acknowledge it as a blessing then all of a sudden veils are lifted and opportunities for growth are presented.

There is a thought process in our collective to push through and move stuff to the side, stay positive and those things are all extremely beneficial. Yet, I think it's also beneficial to be able to sit in sludge, the darkness, the heaviness, and begin to see it as a blessing. The blessing is a teaching aid to mastering your mojo. The experience you are experiencing is what makes you, YOU....Own it.

Why is that? The most precious gems are protected by grit.

All your perceived faults, short comings, issues are all the grit. Acknowledging them and blessing them reveals the gems. This mastering your mojo guide draws on your creative energies to acknowledge your dark spaces and bless them. When I can start to look at myself, or experience/scenario in this way it will open up realms of understanding.

This will also activate authentic success. In this Collective, a Man's success is perceived in a certain way.

Think about it… when you hear the word success what comes to mind first?…What did you visualize first? For most, the visualization shows them a house, car, frolicking in some vast land, or on a beach. Is that the only version of success? Of course not, yet most will have that image.

Acknowledging and blessing your dark spaces and experiences will open your authentic way to knowing your worth and expanding your vision of success. We perceive that if someone is successful that that's the way to do something and in reality that is false.

The person that you see that is "successful" settled into their worth and authenticity. And in this sense, the worth and authenticity is how they serve themselves and how they serve others. I acknowledge that now. I bring this up because we can see something as a success and that can put us in a box and put blinders on, so now we only see one-way rather than using our entire vision and senses around us to really take in what's going on, then create from there.

Take Off Your Blinders

Blinders are thoughts, blinders are feelings, blinders are stories, blinders are influences, blinders are family, blinders are your inner thoughts. I think you get the idea. So to truly acknowledge you as a blessing, take the blinders off of what we think something is, especially what and who you think you are.

There are a lot of perceptions and expectations of a man that are part of a collective consciousness and a collective unconsciousness, then add in conditioning and programming. An example is, the man box… men are supposed to be stoic and stern. Men show strength at all times rather than any sign of weakness. Men pick up the tab and provide, and Men are aloof and insensitive and never listen. I could go on and on, and I think you get the idea, and have most likely heard your own version of a Man Box

Until you find that the box you are in is aligned to someone else's vision, you will continue to live someone else's dream. So for now, let's step out of the box and in to a space to open up to everything around us which is part of Mastering your mojo. Mastering Your Mojo involves connecting to all of our senses in your acknowledging all of who you are.

What does that mean?

Our senses include feeling, smelling, hearing, touching. So where do you fit in in those spaces? For example, how do you feel about yourself, and how do you make people feel?

What are the words you hear yourself say to yourself and what do you hear yourself say to others. As you move through life what do you sense in yourself and what do you sense in others. What are the ways you touch yourself and touch others. Please note, this applies specifically to physical, spiritual, and emotional connection.

As I embraced these questions for myself, I got clarity on the box I created for myself. And to be clear, for me to get that clarity meant asking others how I made them feel, how I spoke to them because I live in a box and can fail to see what really exists.

Begin exploring this space Men and then once you do, you can begin to claim your worth.

Claim Your Worth.

Are you aware of your worth? And before we get into that, what does worth mean to you?

From my own personal life experience, sitting in Men's circles, and leading Men's circles, I find that a difficult challenge for many Men is acknowledging their worth.

Worth is value, which shows up as impact, the way a person influences an environment, and freedom. If you are a Man that makes an impact on and / or influences growth, you are worth something. When was the last time you acknowledged your worth. You see my Guys, part of our alignment to our mission, goal, or purpose is how we align to our worth.

This has been a challenge for most of my life; truthfully, it continues to be a challenge as I develop and level up. I pushed acknowledging my worth to the side for most of my life, and it looked like an excessive amount of volunteer work, being of service, and lowballing whatever services I offered to others.

Sound familiar? Does this resonate? Do you have a way you push off acknowledging your worth?

This topic came front and center when I asked one of my older brothers, Wayne, to mentor me in business development. At the time, I owned and solely operated a cold-pressed juice business and was coaching a couple of men.

In my opinion, Wayne has a solid way of delivering feedback and speaks the plain truth. I knew it was time to finally acknowledge my worth when he gave me feedback on a service I was offering, and the feedback offered was, "Paul, you're undervaluing your services." In his feedback, I really heard, "Paul, you're undervaluing YOURSELF." Wayne did share that feedback with me later in that conversation and others.

At that moment, I recognized I wanted to defend myself, then realized I'd be defending my low self-worth. And the feeling of defensiveness (anger, fear, and shame) was the confirmation that I undervalue myself, and now someone outside of myself acknowledges it.

My next step now that I acknowledged my low self-worth is to bless the parts of myself that have brought me to this point. The defense I sensed was defending something precious, and that something precious is what I get to unearth to realign and rewire a belief or story at the root of "I have low self-worth."

I know from my practices and lessons that I get to get underneath my conscious beliefs and get to their roots. The best way I knew to do that was through Shaman journey work. To dive in, there is a threshold for me to pass through to get to my truth.

"This threshold is a symbol...of passing from the life you know to the unfamiliar".

"I warn you ...do not cross unless you are truly ready to do whatever it takes to get what you came here for".
Paul R. Newell

Moving Through
Your Threshold

Are you ready?

If the answer is no, I respectfully invite you to hone in and practice the methods in the Step Into the Arena section. If Yes, Welcome to Your Threshold

When I learned about principles and tools of Shamanism, I was fascinated at the possibilities and skeptical that they were valid. I remember my first Shaman journey that was guided by an older Gentleman named John, and he invited us to imagine a root, or hole in the ground to go to what he called "The Lower World". I imagined a hole and he led us on the vision of moving down to the Lower World, and he advised us that at some point there is a threshold for you to move through.

I can vividly remember in the journey moving through my threshold that was a viscous slimy consistency. When I moved through it, on the other side was another World. I remember I was in awe of the what I was seeing, and even more odd at the time, was what I was feeling in that World.

That was my first experience with a Threshold, and once a person moves through a threshold, there's no going back to the way things were.

In life, and in the development of the human psyche within the masculine blueprint, there will always be transitions, level ups, shifts in life and in spirit that may be brought on consciously or unconsciously. I write "consciously or unconsciously" because a path of development can look like you taking on a new job opportunity, or diving into a new relationship. You CHOOSE those next steps.

A path of development can also look like you being in an accident, losing your job, or developing a dis-ease. Those things are out of your control...or are they?

You see my Friend, both are paths of development and BOTH are results of conscious and unconscious choices. When I moved through my threshold and explored the realms and roots for the results in my life, it was a powerful and potent experience.

This Threshold is spiritual...it's energetic, and whether we realize it or not, getting to the roots of various matters in our life can be revealing and emotionally charging. This method of moving through a threshold is giving yourself permission to enter a space of that will awaken your imagination, unearth your intentions, and transmute stories and beliefs.

91

Moving through the threshold facilitates an activation of trust. Your mind may telling you, "don't go forward", yet your Heart and Soul are screaming, "it's your time, let's go". this is the depth and potency of approaching the threshold and moving through it..

In the book King, Warrior, Magician, Lover by Robert Moore and Douglas Gillette explore the archetypes of the masculine psyche, and if you have yet to know this book,I highly suggest you read it at least one time. That book, along with being initiated through the Mankind Project, taught me about archetypes, or as I like to call them, Blueprints, and the one that continues to fascinate me, is the blueprint of the magician or mystic. In this book I will use the term Mystic to describe this energy.

The mystic has always been a blueprint that's called to me and I think it's because in my earlier experiences growing up I had to, or I taught myself how to wear masks and show up in ways that were conducive to my environment. I've been a people pleaser for most of my life, and still have to practice focusing on pleasing self first before focusing on pleasing others. My reason for wearing masks and pleasing people was to be safe, accepted, and loved.

In essence I created characters based on what I felt from others. It was never anything tangible, it was a feel...an energy, that I had to draw from to figure out who to be and how to move. To me, that meant having a slight of hand with my psyche. I could observe or scan who someone is and what they wanted, and have an idea of what they're looking for, then I could create a mask to be accepted or to be safe.

This mystic energy has the power to transmute and get men to connect to a deeper part of themselves that has never been tapped into.

This section of mastering your mojo specifically is about embracing a mystical and creative part within you. This mystical creator within you has the ability to transmute old ways and patterns that you uncovered in Step in to the Arena, and begin to transmute them to create something powerful and aligned in your life. These chapters that are coming up after this are about stories, experiences, activities and exercises that you can do to master your mojo and step into that mystic energy within you.

So you may be thinking, why do this, what's the benefit? If this is something that you're thinking, thank you and you're in the right place.

The benefits of doing this will support a man in learning to create something, and to materialize a dream in our physical collective. The ability for man to truly create and step into a powerful dream is something that is usually lacking in the masculine energy because there's a Man box that deters Men from creative activities. It's the box that has boys select sports over music and art. There tends to be some sort of condition or standard for how Men are supposed to show up and engage in society, and that's bullshit.

So are you ready? Are you truly ready to step through the threshold to embrace the mystical creator in you? If so, there's one person you have to go through to get there, and that's your Guardian.

The Guardian

There is something about the term guardian that just activates this powerful and resonant energy in me. I first felt this energy when I was asked to be the "Guardian of the Threshold" in a Men's initiation weekend hosted by the non-profit organization All Kings. Once I heard the title I was already energized to do this role and be of service to the men that were going to come though and be a part of this initiatory weekend.

I remember the first time I held that role and I was being coached on the energy of the role and how to manage that role. I was guided to be like granite, and look deeply into a man's eyes, have him see his reflection, and have the Man in front of me feel the weight of his decision to move into something unknown. I took the role seriously because the Men coming thorough the initiatory weekend had either been in jail/prison, were in danger of going in, or were set to be Mentors and Facilitators for future weekends.

As part of the learning process, someone got to be a Guardian of the Threshold for me, and when I experienced it, I sunk into this feeling that I was about to enter something serious, revealing, and mysterious.

I began to recall the spaces where someone has been a Guardian of a Threshold for me that led into a new experience, and the Guardian came in various forms. They have been a Justice of the Peace when I got married, a future boss before getting a new job, even my surgery to replace my hips. You may not know what the next phase will truly be because deep down you know you're about to change and shift. You don't know what it's going to be like, it's an unknown, yet you also know, whatever is beyond the threshold, it's what's next.

So how does this relate to mastering your mojo? Well, I'm glad you're thinking that.

For any Man to begin to master their mojo, it's a must to be willing to move through something you resist; move into an unknown to tap in to the mystical and creative energy that you possess. It's imperative for us to meet the guardian of the threshold which is ourselves. Yes, the guardian of the threshold is YOU because what's beyond YOU is unknown. Most of the boxes in a Male blueprint are based on our thought and physical process rather than from our senses to determine if our environment is safe. And in most cases there is a safety that people yearn to feel, although in reality safety is a thought that assesses risks and liabilities. Over time we all as humans begin a live from that place, and are free of living on instinct and unseen internal guidance.

Take a moment to ponder the threshold in your life that you get to pass through, or that you resist passing through. Write it down, speak it, claim it.

What is the feeling you have thinking of it? Where is the feeling settling in your body?

I invite you to move into and through your sensations and feelings to explore a fertile and mystic space to create what you want, dream what you desire, and manifest your aligned life.

In this space, practicing intentionality is key because what we think, feel, want and see carry weight in the words we speak to ourselves and others.

"Words have energy and power with the ability to help, to heal, to hinder, to hurt, to harm, to humiliate, and to humble." - Yehuda Berg

Symbols and Spells

After my mom and dad got divorced, my dad was very angry and I can remember my mom felt like my Dad was doing something dark to her. In the Jamaican culture there's something called obeah, which is a kind of source-ery practiced in the Caribbean. While I can neither confirm or deny My Dad practiced it, I could definitely sense something different about my Dad. I would feel that energy intensely when he was expressing his anger toward my Mom. He would say, she's evil, she's a bitch, she's no good, and that's when I felt a dark energy intensely.

He scared me because I never knew when his anger would go over the top. This is when I wore one of my mask to be a good boy and not say anything or be disobedient because I never wanted his anger taken out on me.

My fascination with Obeah really peaked when I went to Jamaica for the first time with my Dad. I was going with my Dad to meet my Aunties, my Uncle, and Cousins on my Dad's side. Now around that time I remember my Dad's words towards and about my Mom had a distinct vitriol to it. The crazy part of this scenario is that my Mom was in a horrible accident where she was sideswiped at a major intersection, while we were in Jamaica. The accident was really bad, and it's a miracle that she and her passenger survived it.

I'm unsure if this happened because my Dad was close to a power source in Jamaica that amplified his words and intentions. And, I do think, with the words my Dad spoke, he contributed to the accident.

Over the years since then, as I heard My Dad say terrible things about my Mom, I grew to hate him, and it all came to a boiling point when we got into a heated argument when I was in my 20's. I was so pissed at him because he failed to show up at my college graduation because my Mom was there. I had enough of his bullshit and I let him have all my rage that I experienced him direct towards my Mom.

I cursed at him and called him out on his words and his anger, and all the things he's said about my Mom. And to wrap it up, I exploded with the words, "I wish you were DEAD!!!!"

I can still remember saying those words along with feeling angry sensations that I created a powerfully intentional spell. Similar to throwing a big rock in a still lake, it's going to create some ripples. I would pass him on the street and fail to acknowledge him, walk past him as if he didn't exist. In my judgment, the words I spoke resonated because several months later he was dead.

Since then, I have been particular with my practice of the words I use and how I use them. Since he's been gone I go back to that moment when I said what I said, and wish I could take it back.

I say this because years later, I learned about my Dad's life, his pains, his struggles, and I also learned that around the time I said I wished he was dead, he was also rejected by some members of his family. So what does that have to do with anything?

Well, he heard words that damaged his sense of worth, and even though he would have never admitted that, I could sense his body gave out from lack of love, and resistance to be loved.

Words have power, and words with intention cast spells.

I bring this up because as I've gotten older, and learned practices like yoga, shaman journeying, Reiki, and sound healing, I've realized the powers of vibration and its impact on our cells. I recognize that the words that we speak carry a vibration and they can impact thoughts, feelings, and actions.

When I was attuned to Reiki Levels 1 & 2, I got to learn symbols to promote various types of energy clearings. I was fascinated by the symbols because when I used them, I could feel differences in myself and feel shifts in others. I move my fingers and hands to create a symbol in the air or on something, and energy would flow to the recipient. As my learning continued, I learned I could do Reiki with out symbols and go solely on intention. And this my Friends blew my mind! This also opened my path to the responsibilities of applying this to knowledge to other areas of life, like my communication.

The fascinating thing about this, is the words that we speak, the sentences that we utter, have impact more than we realize. This guide of Mastering Your Mojo is focused on your language and the intentions in your words. As a Man in this collective environment, I fail to see spaces for Men to learn and practice the art of communication. Men are seen as Leaders, yet most Men lack the tools to be an effective, engaging and influential Leader. This matters because without tools, force is applied rather than skill. This is a result of a dominant patriarchal mindset.

Think about it, in those moments when you think you are misunderstood or failing to connect on a matter, what are the emotions and actions that come up?

For me in those moments, my emotions are anger, rage, sadness, and my actions are detachment, distancing, defending and convicting. Those all have a negative impact on my end game, and my end game is connection, understanding and peace.

I've experienced those emotions and actions dealing with the Mothers of my Children (MOC), especially my former Wife. Throughout the years, I have had to work on my communication because I had tendencies to hold things in until I exploded. Then I would distance myself in shame because I acted in ways that were out of alignment with how I wanted to show up as a Man, a Father, and a Co-Parent.

And with all my work there are still moments where I slide into old ways of communication.

In communicating with the MOC, I slowly started recognizing the anger and vitriol my Dad had towards my Mom is the same energy I was spewing and expressing towards them. And it was painful, destructive, acidic, and disempowering to them, to our bond, and to me. I knew something had to change, although at the time, I had yet to know what that was.

Be Impeccable with Your Word.

Words we speak matter for what happens outside of us, also happens inside of us.

We all can use a language level up. That's right, a language level up.

A language level up is enhanced skill and ability to be present, discerning, descriptive, and direct in your communication. I was opened up to language enhancement when I worked with one of my coaches and mentors John Tompkins. As I write this, I reflect and think on how grateful I am that John was in my life during a time of me transmuting and shifting.

I was in a confused state, recovering from divorce and two soured relationships that produced two kids. Basically, I was in a fucked up place mentally and emotionally. When I met John and we started working together, it was a great time for me to learn new ways to develop myself and rebuild myself in mind, body, and spirit.

John was the author of "Not Crazy Yet?...Then...Start Talking to Yourself Differently" and it's a layout of

Green Language. John's green language is a way of speaking to self and others to rewire the brain to reduce stress and uncertainty in language and communication.

Looking back on working with John, it was a lot like an apprentice working with a master, or guru. It was a lot of uncomfortable mental experiences because in John's way of teaching and rewiring me, it was a lot of interruptions, corrections, reframes in the moment, on the spot. I had a couple blowups at John, and through it was frustrating at times, truth be told, it shifted me and changed me, and I felt it in my body and mind, that how I heard things, how I said things, shoot, even how I saw things, changed.

Men, below are several Language Level-up strategies that will improve the way to speak to yourself and the way you speak to others.

1. **It Starts with Intention:** As I learned in my Reiki practice and training, the healing begins

with intention. This will have you practice your self awareness and really think about the reasons and roots behind your communication. In dealing with my anger and resentment toward my former wife, my intentions in my communication were to create chaos, call her out, and prove her wrong. So with those feeling and thoughts, how do you think the conversations went?

Before you use this strategy is useful in contentious situations; you get to practice regular situations and conversations first. Here are questions you can tap into to bring awareness to your intentions in your communication. *What is the result I seek? What is the root of the reason for this communication? What emotions are you experiencing before or as you are communicating?*

2. **Stop "Shoulding" on Yourself:** The word "Should" may be one of the most damaging

words in the English language, yet we use it haphazardly as we give others advice, and as we market to, and "guide" others. In working with John, I learned how destructive that word is to our emotions and minds. Saying "I Should" or "You Should" is shaming yourself and others. It implies that you are wrong, then can bring the emotion of guilt that you are doing, or have done something wrong. When you hear yourself say "Should" switch it for any of the following words/phrases: "I get to", "I can", "I choose to". When you make the reframe you may sense something different in you, and that My Guys is empowerment. The word "should" impacts the mind as well because when one uses the word "should" without a concrete action step, the brain will begin to view this scenario as a threat because it brings on uncertainty. Men, the brain scours our environment for threats, and if it senses one, it begins preparing the body, mind, and spirit to defend itself, run, hide, or blend in. Having conversations from that place will most likely lead to a breakdown in communication.

3. **Express your Bases:** Men it is of extreme importance that we learn our language bases. The bases are knowing and expressing what you WANT, what you THINK, what you SEE, and what you FEEL. **See** (be observant, what do you see) what would a camera capture. **Feel** (feel yourself) Physically, or emotionally in one of these (mad, sad, glad, afraid, shame). **Think** (taking the time to be present with self)How can curiosity over judgement be beneficial, like " What questions could be helpful? **Want/Request** (reflect on what I would like to see happen) Can I say what *I DO WANT,* when I am about to express what *I DON'T WANT.* When you are figuring these bases out for yourself

be mindful of bringing "nots' into this space. These "not configurations" (I can still hearing John saying that phrase in my head), are also damaging because our mind can begin seeing this as a threat because its ambiguous. For example, saying "I don't want to be in a bad relationship". The brain then questions, "well, what do you want?" That uncertainty brings on instability and an unknown that can bring up defenses. To speak in these ways will invite you to get clear on what you see, explore what you feel, an be courageous to state what you think. This is rooted in empowerment to master your mojo and connect to the mystical creator in you to get clear on what you want to envision and manifest in your life.

"Being versus doing is the key to mastering and harnessing sex energy to create something magnificent."
Paul R. Newell

The Weapon Becomes the Wand

In our collective culture, sex sells...It's in everything that we see and drives most of what we do in our culture. Marketing and advertising strategies will include suggestive images in materials to sway you to purchase something or act in a certain way. The fascinating thing about our culture is that as much as sex is glorified, it's vilified. Sex in most cases is viewed to be either functional, dirty, or sacred.

This Sacral energy center is a base energy center in our development as male human beings, This area is said to develop between the ages of eight to 15. For those that are reading this and have yet to know what the sacral energy center is, it's a space on your body between your belly button and your genitals. The energy there is about creativity, sexuality, and sensuality.

I recognize the importance of understanding the power in the sacral energy center and how it can be expressed in and through me. Many times I considered myself a sexual deviant because of judgement from my former wife and lovers on what I liked sexually and the amount of times I wanted sex. Add to that conditioned religious shame about sex and it made for a potent shame elixir. I do my best to be free of judging myself about sex, yet every time I go in a depression and shame spiral, porn is there to console me.

My sex education came from porn and that conditioned me to think women were playthings to go in various positions and do acts like I saw in the porn movies. When I became sexually active, I realized real sex was nothing like the movies. Now Fellas there are some women out there that will perform like the porn stars in the movie and chances are she may not be the best partner for a life long relationship. And yes I'm judging.

Looking back on it, I think that my porn consumption damaged a lot of relationships I've had, and it's a practice for me to be conscious during sexual activity, in how I am present during sex and how I work with my sexual energy as method of pleasing and healing myself. I started settling into the power of the energy center in my physical health when I was working with an energy worker, Ilona. Ilona supported me in clearing my energies and to get my body and spirit ready for a double hip replacement surgery. Along the way, she provided guidance on ways to tune in to my energy center's wisdom.

In one of our sessions, she cleared out my Sacral energy center, and as she was doing that, I could see women I have slept with over the years leaving my body. It was surreal!!! Some of the women that were leaving

I didn't even recognize and others I wanted to stay and found myself grabbing for them and they became ghosts as soon as I could touch them. I got to understand the attachment energetically I've made through sex and how those energies were in and around me.

That session with Ilona planted a seed of what is possible and what's been a reality. The reality was that I was using sex as a deterrent, a pacifier, when I was resistant to dealing with life circumstances for years. I was lustful and focused on smashing something to feel better, and in almost all of those experiences, I felt even worse afterward. Reflecting on those experiences, I realized I used my dick as a weapon. It was my tool to conquer my problems, my tool to sway and engage with sexual partners, and my tool of self-destruction.

This became clear to me during my sex detox to identify and clear out old stuff and stories about sex and my connection to it. Most of what I learned about sex, I learned from porn. I've gotten feedback about my sex "performance", and in those experiences it was about getting in positions, or exploring how wet I could get a woman either through tasting, touching, or fucking. It became a game that was really a distraction.

During my sex detox I became aware of how sex is communicated in our collective culture. For example there phrases like:

- Beat that p***y up

- Gimme that p***y

- Take that d**k in your p***y

When I thought about words I've said to women, I could visualize the transactional physical expression of anger and sadness through sex over the years.

This my Friend is programming for sexual violence. This may be heavy for some to receive, and in the heat of lust and passion, primal energies can come up and we can say some things. The sexual violence I write of is about how we view our sex organ and what our intentions are with it.

If how you have sex is out of alignment with what you want I invite you to explore what you say about sex. How do you view your sex organ? Do you love it or despise it? And would your actions towards your sex organ support your response? As I asked myself these questions, something activated in me. Reflecting back, I realize that was an activation of mature sex energy.

I came to terms with the fact that my nuts carry potent seeds, so I got snipped (vasectomy). My curious self explored what could I create with the potency of my seeds. That's when I knew this could be the spark to get my book done. That's also when I thought to myself that I'm going to turn my dick into a wand.

To do that, I went and got advise from one of the original deans of development, Napoleon Hill.

The Mystery of Sex Transmutation.

"*Sex desire is the most powerful of human desires . When driven by this desire, people develop keenness of imagination, courage, will power, persistence, and creative ability unknown to them at other times... When harnessed and redirected along others lines, the positive attributes of this motivating force may be used as powerful creative forces in literature, art or in any other profession or calling , including, of course, the accumulation of riches. - Napoleon Hill from Think and Grow Rich*

I've read Think and Grow Rich many of times and failed to take in that message. I finally decided to dive into sex transmutation when I re-set a goal to write and finish the book. I write "re-set" because I made the book a goal in 2021 and failed to complete it. The year of 2022 was the year I was going to get it done and I knew I needed extra umph to get this done, and sex transmutation was it.

To do this, I created a program for myself to support me in getting dick discipline. Having a program called dick discipline was a stretch for me. I am a recovering people pleaser so a lot of my life has been about making sure that whatever I do or say is a good reflection of who I am as a person or how I'm perceived.

Dick discipline is a space that I created for men to claim something that they want and teach themselves how to leverage their powerful potent sexual creative mystical energy to create something from their vision. Create and manifest something special on this journey that will provide them with the tools and insights within themselves to create something powerful.

The key piece from the dick discipline journey was to master the alluring and potent sexual energy that resides in my body and balls. The thing that becomes dangerous is when that attraction to sexual energy becomes destructive and distracting. I perceive that our collective uses sex in a destructive, and dominating manner to create disconnection from self and others.

The cool thing about this experience was doing the dick discipline with other Men over a 12 week period. Some Men eventually fell off, while there were a few that stayed on to the end.

In the first leg of the experience, I was mindful of my urges for sex, porn, and jerking off. That is when I recognized my patterns to turn to those things when experiencing sadness, depression, or anger. I felt some anxiety as I went without and recognized how much I was relying on porn for stimulation.

There were some times that I slipped and watched porn and I was shocked at the violence in the movies. I recognized in watching porn I was conditioning myself to view my dick as a weapon. At that point I made a title reframe in the middle of the program and refrained from calling my penis a "dick" and began calling it a "lingham".

> *Lingam, (Sanskrit: "sign" or "distinguishing symbol") also spelled linga, in Hinduism, an object that symbolizes **the god Shiva** and is revered as an emblem of generative power.*

So during the disappointing moments when I had connection with my lingam and just massaged myself without pornographic material it was a stretch for me because I was relying on that visual stimulant to get me excited. I had to retrain myself to really sense what was going on in and for my body. Activating sensuality within my body has many benefits because it's a way of getting more present with everything in my environment and a great way of getting present with what's happening with my physical body.

I became aware of what's happening with my attention. What gets me aroused? What does that feel like, look like, and sound like? What happens with my breath? Is there tension in my body? And where is it?

In the western culture, there's very little time carved out for us to feel, sense, and be, especially sexually. It's sold that sex is quick…insert your member here, bust a nut, go to sleep. And sex is more than that. This took hold when I shifted my mindset to view my penis as a wand rather than a weapon.

Me spilling my seed all over the place resulted in my having two other kids with two different women. I rarely see those kids because my relationship with their mothers was transactional. There was no REAL love there and over time it was evident to me with their actions to move the kids away from their father.

This scenario happens to a good number of men. Men and women have sex unconsciously, a baby is born and a life time of conflict, turmoil, and emotional dis-ease usually ensue. We think with our dick and get ourselves into trouble. Are having kids' trouble? No. Trouble is having a contentious relationship with a co-parent.

Even in the discomfort of contentious relationships with the mothers of my children, it opened up a portal of forgiveness for self and my "dick". The ways I abused it, and the ways it abused, the results from carelessness, shame, and throw anger in the mix too. This level of awareness opened me up to what has constricted my mojo all along…My Wounds.

"Our sorrow and wounds are healed only when we touch them with compassion."

Buddha

Lay Down Your Wounds

Whatever circumstance(s) a man is in, that he wants to move past or through, it is a must that they lay down any wounds that come up in their quest for the next level. My buddy Les Gaines and I recorded a conversation a couple of years before he passed on. We were discussing the concept of dropping the walls, and defenses, and laying down our wounds.

Being initiated into the New Warrior training adventure in 2014 was an experience of me learning more about masculine energy. I got the opportunity to explore what it was like to have masculine guidance from men. I experienced what it was like to be nurtured by Men and what I also found in that space is that the masculine nurturing is more rigid and raw. My perspective that it was necessary for men in those stages of initiation, transitioning to a new way of being required a rigid, raw, and direct space. I bring this up because healing wounds is about dropping the stories and beliefs, then dropping in.

In that call with Les when he was speaking from an Elder or Older Guide perspective on addressing someone's wounds and stories, he said the words,

"Hey, are you done crying about your story, about your situation?....OK now drop it."

The manner in which he said it activated me and I sensed my body tense up. I got the sense in those words that my experience was disregarded. At that point, I made the statement to lay down the wound so it can be honored and revered, and embraced as sacred so it can pass on and heal to plant new seeds for new flowers and experiences.

Laying down my wounds and my patterns that grew from them was a difficult space for me, and still can be. One of things to notice and acknowledge in the realm of self-development is that there is always work that can be done. I say can be done because it's truly up to the person if they are in the space to truly explore, and if it's a space that they are truly willing to let go of. This was my issue when I revisited the exercise of laying down wounds using the shamanic ritual/practice I learned when I was in a sacred Shaman mentorship.

I made this an activity in the Dick Discipline Experience. I asked Men to get a rock, trace it on a piece of paper and then write down what it is that they are burying. What it is they were laying down... letting go of...setting free?

Little did I realize how impactful that exercise was going to be for me. For me, I lay down the wounds of the cuts and scars I perceived and experienced from the mothers of my children. I lay down the wounds in my heart from wanting to have a relationship with my kids and failing to. The wild thing about this was that I allowed myself to let it all come to the surface, everything that I was hiding, everything that I kept behind my mask, and everything that I kept bottled up to make everything nicely nice while I was severely damaging myself inside.

When I wrote those things down, I also recognized how angry I was about my situation, and how much I wanted to correct how much I was resenting the mothers of my kids. After I settled into that, the tough thing was that it was difficult for me to even let go and bury the rock because I had become so attached to that pain or discomfort, that uneasiness, that I was unsure of who I would be without it. So, I procrastinated because a part of me wanted to be in that space. As if I deserved to be there.

Those scenarios had a hold on me, and played a role in how I was living my life, the thoughts that I was moving into and through, as well as my perceptions of things. This activity in Dick Discipline brought light to my patterns in regards to how much I was bottling in, how much I acted as if it didn't matter, and how much I act stoic and that everything is OK. In reality, I was fucking pissed off, angry, sad, and wanted to take somebody's fucking head off! I wanted justice.

And now that I acknowledge that, I get to lay it down. I get to move into and through it. I get to complete this hurt, this trauma that's been bubbling in my veins and energy for years.

Why does this matter when it comes to mastering your mojo?

It matters because for Men, for you and me, to be our most authentic selves, we get to lay our wounds down because when we fail to lay them down, we live through them. We act from them and that is a victim mentality source that disconnects us from our best selves.

When we lay down the wound, we complete a trauma and then the wound becomes a teacher and guide for who we are and how we show up.

Please process the activity for this method:

- *What are the hurts and pains you are willing to lay down and set free?*

- *What is the area, scenario, person, or thing in your life that has had its hooks in you and dominates you emotionally, physically, mentally, spiritually, or socially? What is that one thing; what is that scenario?*

Laying it down isn't dropping it and making it a bad thing. Laying it down is putting it away with honor, respect, reflection and introspection. By doing that, that wound becomes a guide to your best and highest self.

An Invitation to Rise Into Your King

Drawing by Paul Newell

"I am, indeed, a King, because I know how to rule myself. ..."

Pietro Aretino

What does it mean to be a King? What are the characteristics of a King?

Sovereign King is based on the King archetype described by Carl Jung. Carl Gustav Jung (July 26, 1875 – June 6, 1961) was an influential psychologist who established the field of analytical psychology. Jung is known for his theorizing about the human unconscious, including the idea that there is a collective unconscious all people share. According to Jung the qualities of a King include:

- He is centered
- He is decisive
- He lives with integrity
- He protects his realm (family, friends, community)
- He provides order
- He creates and inspires creativity in others
- He leaves a legacy.

It can mean self-exploration and self-activation. An internal capacity to manage self and grow the various domains (health, finances, career, social, and relationships) in your life in a healthy way that nourishes yourself and your people (those you love and cherish).

The word 'king' can have a negative connotation in our culture. King can be thought of as a tyrant, a destructive ruler that can be dominant and unethical. I often wonder what the reason is. I mean, there have been good kings in the existence of humanity. The first one that comes to mind is King Solomon. If you're a bible reader, you also know King Solomon turned sour in his reign.

King, in this context, is sovereign energy and leveraging internal wisdom and experience to make decisions. This all came to my head after going through about six to seven weekends of staffing new warrior training adventure for the Mankind Project. These weekends were ripe spaces for learning more about these energies of a King, along with the energies of a Lover, a Warrior, and a Magician.

I can remember thinking kings are dominant and tyrannical and destined for corruption. That's conditioning. A King is much more that a Man sitting on his throne barking orders. A King rules over many domains and to do that, he has to have experienced being a lover, being a warrior, being a Mystic to know how those blueprints are represented in him.

Most people fail to see the rise to that sovereign energy and what it takes to get there.

So, this practice that we're doing here is slowly unraveling who you are and how you are designed to authentically show up. The kingdom I speak of, or the King's domain, have different aspects of life that have yet to create harmony in your life.

Men, harmony is a key for us to rise into our sovereign energy from our heart. Rising into the sovereign energy requires that we harmonize with other energies that are in us, such as how we love, how we care for ourselves and others, how we create new beginnings, and how we live in child-like play.

To fully access and integrate these guides that follow, it is important that you embrace a couple of realms. One is the realm of your body, the other is the realm of your love.

Men, I invite you to level-up and step into your Sovereign self.

A King's Body

From my experience, the big stuff in life (grand goals, mission, and vision) require a vessel(s) to manifest it or fulfill it. My curiosity gets the better of me wondering if Men realize we are born with a vessel to fulfill our mission and dreams.

All humans are gifted a body, and my judgement is few recognize the magnificence of the gift given.

First, I will own that I have viewed my body as a utilitarian device; something to get from point A to point B in whatever way it needs too. As I enter my mid-forties, I feel the impact of viewing my body that way, and I've chosen to experience and treat my physical form in a different way.

I have committed to experiencing my body as an **instrument, an investment,** and an **asset**. All these components have been inserted into the Rise Into Your King guide because for a man to step fully into his realm, he gets to have awareness of his primary realm, his body.

To help me create my programming, I found myself asking the following questions regarding my body and how I perceive it.

My Body as an Instrument...

Let's first define the term "instrument". Most are familiar with its definition as a tool for work or expression. For the purpose of this King's Guide, its definition is a device used to gauge a level or something. To appreciate the body as our vessel, its imperative we become aware of what is happening with our bodies.

Questions for Reflection:

- How am I using my body as an instrument for my mission?

- What does my body tell me that I have been resistant to hear?

- What do I get to do to refine my body as an instrument?

Investing in our Body for the Highest Good

I'm learning that for my body to be in peak performance, resources will be invested. Resources can range from money to time and energy. To keep this simple for me and us all, let's focus on three major investments that Men can make in their bodies.

Questions for Reflection:

- What are the ways I invest in my body?
- When was the last time I invested in my body, and what was the exchange?
- What investment will I make in my body to work toward my mission?

My Greatest Asset...is ME!

Yes, this is true...take that in. You are your greatest asset, I am my greatest asset. By definition, an asset is a useful or valuable thing. Asset is also defined as property owned by a person that is regarded as having value and available to meet debts, commitments, or legacies.

As Kings we are creating our legacies, and the body is one of assets available to make it reality.

Questions for Reflection:

- What are the ways my body is an asset?

- What are the ways I will treat my body as an asset?

Take some moments to reflect on one or a couple of these questions. Do your best not to reflect on all questions in one setting. Allow yourself the space for responses to rise from within you.

****

A King's Love

"Do You Love Yourself?

My heart became as heavy as an anchor as it sunk into my stomach when I read that line in the passage.

Well, do I love myself? And what does that even mean? Like a Man in this life, I was never taught what loving myself is or what it can be. As I continue working with Men, I find other men experience the same thing.

I was conditioned unconsciously and consciously about love for another. You know the flowers, the hugs, the kind words, or gifts. And when I recollect the ways I was taught to love, I recognized that I'm doing none of those things for myself. So this presents the opportunity to learn and create a model for myself. And as it works for me, I can share with others.

To begin this model, I get to create a foundation to build this. As I set that intention, the source became clear.

Divine intervention places a written piece of work from Harold R. Nelson, titled "First, Love Yourself!" As I read this piece, I became enamored with its content and the guidelines it provided me. It provided the guidance I was looking for to create my self-love model for myself and the other Kings coming up.

So, gentlemen, I present to you the three stages of Self-Adoration and activities for reflection.

Guide 1: Learning Who You Are (Self-Awareness)

Harold R. Nelson wrote, "If I am to love myself, I must know what I am and am not." This step is about looking at all of myself and I mean "ALL" of myself. The "good", the "bad", and "indifferent"; and in reality, who I am is none of those things, I am.

The conditioning of masculinity has us thinking we are less than if we are angry, sad, or abrupt. We are then sold the mirage of being a good boy (man), which unconsciously has us judging the various parts of ourselves as either good or bad.

Activities for Reflection:

- Create a list of 10 things that are "good" about you (feel free to get feedback from family, friends, etc).

- Create a list of 10 things that are "bad" about you (feel free to get feedback from family, friends, etc).

- Create a list of 5 - 10 things that are "different" about you. (TIPS: these may be traits, thoughts, beliefs, activities that you seldom share with others)

Guide 2: Bless It All (Self-Acceptance)

In Mr. Nelson's piece, he states, "self-acceptance is closely tied with the capacity to receive forgiveness of my sins." I took the liberties of shifting "sins" to "self".

After reading this and integrating the phrase into my reflections, I began to see that underneath my thoughts and behaviors were projections and judgments on myself that I am bad. That I am bad...even writing that creates a tension in my body. So I practice letting go (of projections and judgments) and forgive myself. And THEN, the self-acceptance of myself flowed.

In our society, there are conditions to being a "Man". Its all around us and starts from the time we are young, and the conditional messages come from the authorities in our lives. Growing up in the that way leaves us (Men) is open space for shame and right and wrong, then leading to feelings/thoughts that, "I'm not enough as I am". And that is a lie.

As we are raised in that way, forgiveness of self is the ultimate permission to be one's self and step fully into a King's love of self. And from THAT place, we can give love to others...

Activities for Reflection:

- Use one of the lists from the previous step. Take one thing at a time and read each item and after each item state, "I receive and accept that about myself".

- As you go through these activities, note thoughts, emotions, stories that are coming up for you. Chances are whatever is coming up has either been waiting to be revealed or has been blocking you from forgiving and accepting yourself completely.

Guide 3: Love Your Realm (Self-Giving)

Following self-awareness, and self-acceptance open to gates for us to fully love another. In my judgment, this is a teaching Men do hear, and if they hear it, they don't receive it.

I can't even begin to tell you how many times I've heard, "I want you to be more loving…", or "I don't feel that you love me". Those terms would frustrate me to no end because I thought, I was doing "loving" acts; and the deeper question, "loving" for who?

I had in my mind what loving can be and is and reflecting on this has me recall that I never had a base to love from. When a man loves himself, he can be patient with himself. He can be kind to himself. He can connect with himself. All of these are solid grounds for loving others right? Patience, kindness, connection.

By having love for self fully and authentically, we can give and have love for others that is not based on conditions and judgment; it's based on heart and truth.

Activities for Reflection:

- Create a list of 10 new ways you can authentically show love to self

- Create a list of 10 new ways another can authentically show love to you

- Embrace these activities of reflection, and my invitation is to experience the activities in the order they are presented. I want you to take the path of resistance for it will craft the road to your Kingdom.

Rising Into Your King is not about learning anything new, its about remembering all of who you are and then applying to it various realms in your life (aka Kingdom).

"Remember who you are..."

Ramonda (from Black Panther)

Go To The Roots

In order for a man to truly claim the crown, they have to go into the roots. In this case the roots are our history, our lineage, our lines. Our line contains keys and gems to help manage our realms and domains.

In order to do this, we get to do energy center work and we started to cover that a bit in Step into the Arena. We got a handle on who we are, our patterns, beliefs, and stories. Those patterns, beliefs and stories come from our root energy center otherwise known as the root chakra. The root energy center is the space for security, stability and structure.

If you think about the term root, and looking at a diagram of the energy centers along the spine, the Root chakra is at the base of the spine, which provides structure for all the other energy centers and it physically provides structure for how our spine aligns later in life.

For men our root and sacral energy centers are blocked, damaged or underdeveloped. This results in infantile behavior, tyrant behavior, dominant sexual behavior, and uncertainty in regards to sexuality and how to express ourselves creatively, sensually. One of the biggest things for men in regards to claiming their sovereignty, is creativity.

Now the fascinating thing about this is that creativity is known to be a feminine trait. And however you view it, I'm detached, I'm more concerned that most men fail to step into creativity. Why do you think that is?

From young days in a boy's life, our collective consciousness has boys shying away from creative endeavors. What I'm seeing in our collective now is that there are more boys going into manhood that are able to express their creativity, which I think is key to being able to really manage the throne. So let's dive into the roots, and here's the activity in the space provided:

List 10 traits of your lineage on your mom's side and on your dad's side.

Now, this is the area you may have to dig a little bit; you may have to connect to family members, connect to aunts and uncles, go to storyboards, or do your ancestry. Whatever that is for you, it's worth it.

One of the reasons I was inspired to create these methods in regards to a man's health is because for us to really be our full selves, we get to know where we came from, which can apply to men or women. For men, I think it's important for us to understand our ancestry's characteristics, skills, and traits.

The Roots of Worthiness

When I write about going to the Roots of our ancestral lines, it's more about going to the roots of our trauma. In an earlier section of this book, I wrote about knowing your worth. My method to get to the root of my issues with my worth were to go in via shaman journey. Please note your preference to get there can be through therapy, family conversations, hypnosis, whatever works for you is the go to.

I set the intention to connect with the root of my low sense of worth. The journey revealed the repeated mantra of "I'm a worthless piece of shit". At first I heard it repeatedly in my journey, then I could see visions of Men and Women saying it to member's of my family on my Dad and Mom's side.

The voices grew louder, and the vision got clearer until the voices became echos that reverberated in my ancestral lines because of pains, scarcity, and ignorance. Experiencing the roots of my worthiness activated my grace and wisdom of my journey, and begin to receive the messages of worthiness.

The Roots of Teaching

When I was younger the question was asked "What do you want to be when you grow up?"

My response back then was an architect or artist. Now...my response would be a teacher. It's something that has called to me and the more I learned about my lineage the more I understood my love of teaching.

My Granddad on my Dad's side was a teacher and school administrator. My Dad loved researching and writing, my Mom had a knack for making complex things seem simple, and she had a way of figuring out and teaching others to do the same. They gave me a sense of resourcefulness and relatability when I teach.

Success leaves clues and if a Man studies his Family, he will find clues about his path that can awaken strengths. And studying family can provide a run down of lessons that your ancestors experienced that you can learn from.

Leadership is the capacity to translate vision into reality. –

Warren Bennis

Man on Mission

When I was a teenager and watched a lot of sports, I can remember getting chills when I would see an athlete go off in their sport, and the announcer would claim the athlete was on a mission. I think back on it now and realize it's stuck with me because I failed to truly understand what that meant and at the same time understood it completely.

Mission was synonymous with focus, being free of distractions. When I staffed a new warrior training adventure, I really got to connect with Mission and feel it. When I went through the process of creating my mission, I was creating it from who I truly am. For example, what is it that I want to create? What's the kind of world that I want to see? What kind of world do I want my kids to grow up in? Then from that space, realizing what kind of environment I want to create, what are the ways that I do that, what is it in me or what kind of access and resources do I have internally to help me create the kind of world that I want.

After going through the process of creating my mission, I can vividly remember a tension trickling down the top of my head all the way down to my feet. At that moment I knew that this was something serious and that term "a man on mission" resonated deeply.

Having a mission is having a grand vision. When I started going through the process of creating a mission statement and thinking of the world I want to create, and the ways I was going to do that seemed daunting and impossible in my life time. It's key to note a mission you create may come to fruition in a life time beyond yours. You may be the start of, and contributor to the world you are set to co-create. I noticed after I created my first mission statement, it took practice for me to really settle into saying it. I think that's important, it was important for me. The benefit of having this mission when I was going astray and falling off, was to connect to a grander perspective or overview of where I was in my life and it became my north star on how I was going to forward.

As I go through my development, and working with men as they do the same, I realized that many men had yet to claim their mission and settle into it. And what really got me is that most men had a difficult time in claiming what they want.

Men, your ability to claim what you want gives you a path to step into sovereign/King energy.

Why?

In order to reign over your realms like your finances, your relationships, your career, and your fun it's imperative to know what you want. What do you want to create? What do you prefer? What do you want to see? What's your vision?

This is your space, your guide for you to create and align to your mission so let's build it. This is the space to begin to truly settle into what you want, what do you want to create for yourself and your environment. For these activities I want you to step into your confidence and competence and be free of being humble. I want you to get grandiose, brag on yourself and tell the highest details of what you do and how you do it.

Now that we've done that let's start to hone in on what makes you, YOU. This is another area where men may have challenges, bragging about themselves, speaking on their abilities, really acknowledging the things that make them, THEM.

You know what I'm talking about, that unique part of yourself. The thing that you love, adore, and cherish doing. That thing that maybe you would do for free. For me, it's people, it's getting people to find their unique connection to their body, their mind, and their spirit.

Reflection Keys:

What makes you, you?

What is unique about you that you would protect at all costs?

What do you love to do that you would do for free?

Mission Creation

Here is a starting point to creating your mission: (Extracted from the Omega Point Program)

WHAT I WANT MOST: _____
Write it here as a noun: (i.e. Peace):

Now write it as an adjective: _____
(i.e. Peace becomes Peaceful):

Insert this adjective into the statement below (A)

HOW DO I GIVE IT?

Describe how you give what you want using three verbs, write them below and then insert those verbs into the statement below:

(B)

(C)

(D)

INITIAL MISSION STATEMENT:

My Mission is to Create a _____   World / Culture / Society
                          (A) (from above)   (pick one)

by, though, with _____, _____ and _____
    (pick one)   (B) verb   (C) verb   (D) verb

Example: My mission is to create an enlightened culture through healing and teaching.

Write New mission statement here and in Journal:

Claim your mission…go to a mirror say it to yourself, say it to a friend. Say it loud too King!!!

The invitation here Men is to claim your mission every damn day. And so it is.

"It is impossible for a man to learn what he thinks he already knows"

Epictetus

The Master
Knows Nothing

The term master has come to mean a person that has achieved the highest level of a subject, experience, or training. So what a surprise it was to me to hear the phrase, "a mastery knows nothing".

I've heard this before in eastern philosophy texts, however reading it, then integrating that knowledge had become two different things. Reading about it made it a concept to acheive after years of practice with Yoga, Shamanism, and Reiki work. The instilling and integration was a different type of practice that I had yet to know.

Before I get into that, I want to go further into what this concept means and why it's relevant to a man rising into their sovereign energy. To fully embrace sovereign energy is to embrace everything that could be, then create something based on what is. Mastery does mean attaining a certain level of something.

In my yoga journey, I remember going through my 500 hour certification and feeling an accomplishment and, at the same time, feeling a nervousness because I had no idea what having this certification meant in the field. When I got my 500-hour Yoga certification, I had yet to define the way in which I wanted to use it. Now this is where the integration of knowing something in depth brings this statement to life.

My buddy and Reiki Master guide, CA, a.k.a. Carol Anne, said in my Reiki master attunement that mastery is realizing that I know nothing. And I fail to recall who originally said that and at that moment when she said it, especially with Reiki energy healing. It was basically a pass to say, 'explore and integrate what I know with what I have yet to know based on what and who I think I am, and have learned.'

In order for a man to truly rise into a sovereign king energy, a Man gets to forget what he knows, and create something different to achieve another level of learning and understanding. Part of this integration of wisdom is in creation space. What does that mean?

A Beginner's Mind

A couple of years after I completed my 500 hour yoga certification, I was invited to be a yoga teacher trainer facilitator with an emphasis on anatomy and physiology. At the time, there was an outline on what to teach and I was given freedom to create my own content based on eight years prior experience as a personal trainer.

I was touted as an "expert" in the field and that got to my head. I know my prep was subpar, I failed to do a thoroughly review the outline or even organize my thoughts on paper. I thought I could wing it because I have "experience".

WOW, was I wrong and off! That was one of the most uncomfortable teaching moments I've had to date.

That class peppered me with questions because they were curious and I knew some of the answers to their questions and I think I talked shit on some of my answers. Did the class know? Maybe. And whether they knew or not, I felt like shit because I realized I got cocky and didn't know a much as I thought I did.

After that experience, I took on the beginner's mind. I committed to myself that no matter what I think I know, each experience is brand new.

It is important for my self-development that I learn and practice having a beginner's mind. This is important because when I have a concept or thought about how something works, everything will have to work that way. When I surrender and set free all my thoughts, beliefs, patterns, and conditioning, some things I see are far from what I want to see. And when I set those things aside and I'm coming from who I am, then I can truly step into all that is in the moment and decide which path I want to take.

Is this sovereignty? I think it is. It's also taking a step back to see the whole then move, into something rather than rush into it.

Conditioned Masters

Part of rising into sovereign king energy is recognizing the conditioned masters in you. As I learned the lessons of a master know nothing, I began to understand the concept can be applied to the conditioning I grew up in that has been my master and kept me confined.

The conditioning I practiced on was my conditioning around finances. Growing up in my version of a divorced household, money was a sore topic. My Mom would worry about money and be pressed to get child support from My Dad. My Dad would complain to my Mom, he had no money, yet he would carry a wad of cash around. (DISCLAIMER: he owned his own cab business so he had to have cash for change).

The conditioning for money was that money creates chaos and resentment, its evil, and I want no part of it. I began to perceive that people with money were evil and whenever I got money I would blow it. (My unconscious belief, I don't want money because it will change me and will make me evil).

In this instance, I got to observe my conditioned money master as a part of myself that has wants and needs. From that space I get curious and questioned what is another way I can see money? What are other options I can do with money? This method respects the conditioning, then expands it to create a new view and way of being.

Reflection for your Sovereign King:

What do you think you have mastered? Where in that mastery is your space to be a beginner?

What do you think has mastered you? What is you way of creating new conditions from it?

"Surround yourself with people who make you hungry for life, touch your heart, and nourish your soul."

-author unknown

Create Your King's Court

A King's court is a term that describes the king's council and household. A court travelled with the King wherever he went. A King would seek advice from the wise (hopefully) Guides of his court which would include relatives, barons, lords, and members of the church such as bishops.

The first time I heard this term I was fascinated by it and when I looked up what it meant I became even more enthralled with the term. And I believe that each man gets to have their own King's court. Each man can do well with a council of people at his side. The collective wisdom of a council can help a King navigate their version of life in various situations.

What are the areas in your life that you want to improve and dive into? This is where you start; get clear on where you want to go. Next consider who do you get to become to get there. This is potent space because there is clarity and direction. The next parts are about setting up your support system to be your council and accountability along the way.

Energetic Discernment

As I get older, I'm integrating the practice of discernment. I've had tendencies to say yes to everything. I was the Captain of Doublebooking and Flakeouts. I would commit to stuff and forget, then beat myself up when I set no boundaries and failed to say "no". When I dove into that through therapy, I recognized that I went along with everything to be liked, to please others, or to be accepted. I was resistant to asking questions to know more about an opportunity/event and super resistant to say "no". The story I had in my head is like the example below:

"I can't ask them questions because that may make them uncomfortable and then I'll be uncomfortable, and I don't want any conflict."...."If I say no, they may never ask me again." Sure that may read crazy and these are the types of stories that exist in my head that dampened my discernment.

To practice and enhance my discernment, I needed to connect with my energy in three phases:

- Energy Awareness: what are I sensing in my body and where is it?

- Energy Understanding: what activated that energy?

- Energetic Action: what will I do with that energy?

Check Your Environment

Men, when was the last time you assessed the surroundings in which you operate? For anything to succeed, it gets to have the right environment. The collective story of Men going through life alone has Men failing to adjust their surroundings to what they want in life. I'm one of those Guys that will have friends from childhood because we have history, yet those friends are out of alignment with what intend to become. I still have those friends, AND I have new Men in my life that have become a part of my King's Court. Those Men are the ones that inspire me, challenge me and hold me accountable to the big shit I'm up to in my life.

Every Man gets to surround himself with people that will stretch him. For me it's been a combination of friends, mentors, groups, even spirit guides.

Be One of the Guys

"I myself know, no Man is an island, no Man stands alone." Sizzla Kalonji

No Man stands alone regardless of what you hear or are taught. To activate and fully embrace the King within you it's beneficial to be a part of a Men's Circle or Mastermind. A well-run men's group can result in freed up energy for life activities and an expansion of the "toolbox" of interpersonal skills. In a group, men can experience a sense of belonging and closeness that reduces isolation, frustration, and depression.

If you have difficulty finding a Men's circle/group, it may be a message to start your own. Here are some basics to get started:

- **Structure:** Circles are at least 3 men, ideally 8-12 men, and not more than 20 men. Choose a specific venue for the Circle or rotate the meeting every session in a different man's home. Meet once every 2 weeks, or at least once per month, and once circle becomes consistent, some Men can meet once a week. Establish ground rules and agreements of the circle that will be safety, and a judgement-free experience.

- **Topic:** Have an outline of topics for the month and or meeting ahead. This can attract Men to your circle and also engage Men into conversation. Tip: keep topics universal and steer clear of politics and religion, unless either of those are the foundation of your circle.

- **Buddy System:** Have Men connect and check-in with each other outside of the group. Be sure to provide basic guidelines on the check-in, like how long is a check-in? How often do they check-in? What is the structure of the check-in.

These things matter. The masculine energy engages with order so this will appeal to Men on a deeper level. Having this structure enhances trust and safety, which can provide Men with a space to learn and grow.

Reflection: Foundation for Creating YOUR King's Court

Step 1: Claim Your Mission in the space below:

Step 2: What are two of your strengths to nurture and support your mission? (What/who are two resources to work with to practice and enhance these skills)

Step 3: Where / What are two opportunities to grow that will support your missions? (What /who are two people in your circles that can guide you to knowledge and wisdom in these areas)

Step 4: Claim one act/ habit / pattern that could trip you as you work toward your mission? (Who is one person you trust t support you and hold you accountable to keeping this habit / pattern / act in check?

Please note these resources can be people, books, classes, social groups. Tune into what can and will work for you. When you have connected with your resources, I invite you to connect in moderation so you can focus on integrating, and practicing what you learn, rather than constantly learning and consuming more information.

Men, establishing your King's Court will be a key component to you achieving self awareness and fulfillment through growth and healthy challenges. A King's Court is your container to explore yourself free of judgment. All the lessons in this Guide are designed for you to explore yourself, recreate yourself, then rise into your highest self. For you to enhance this lessons and integrate them into your life, have a Court that will support you by holding you accountable to what you say, engaging you to grow, and celebrating your journey along the way.

If every Man could have that, I truly believe our circumstances in our current society would be vastly different.

And so it is, and so it is, and so it is.

Outro

Blessings to you for taking the journey within, and thank you for being willing to receive and process the sections and lessons that preceded this outro.

What have you acknowledged about yourself?

My intention for writing this Method is for me and others to have lessons to return to, and to keep exploring the nuances of who we are. Whatever circumstance(s) you are experiencing in your life, knowing yourself will be at the root of how you perceive and act on the circumstance. Others may support you on your journey to getting to that place, but the last leg of the journey is always yours to go alone. In times of doubt, struggle, evolution, and confidence, be mindful and present and remember who you are.

What have you appreciated about yourself?

I want men to address and appreciate the generative, creative, and often underappreciated feminine energy within. Everything has masculine and feminine properties... EVERYTHING. Appreciating the parts of your spirit and mind that can blossom by harnessing sex energy and practicing disciplines will enhance how we express ourselves as Men. This also shifts the ways to show up and influence our World.

What have you aligned with?

My vision for Men and Masculine energy is that it's aligned with something higher than the physical self. After reading these sections and lessons, that may make sense and if that statement is vague, here is another way I can express it; Men lead themselves on the path that will bring rewards that are expressions of their true selves and that benefit those they touch and connect with. I've witnessed men shift before my eyes when they feel what alignment and direction can be for them. It looks as if they short-circuit or millions of neurons in their physical form and got a surge of electricity all at once.

An Invitation

So what's next for you? Where can you go from here? Hell, where do you WANT to go from here?

I have the tendency to move right on to another thing, and I can fail to allow what I've just taken in to settle in, then allow myself the space and practices to integrate what I've taken in.

I invite you to allow yourself to reflect on these lessons, reread them, and journal on them. Talk to another person about what you've taught yourself about yourself. That other person can be a friend, partner, therapist, or whoever you trust and can be an open, judgment-free space for you to be seen and heard.

My invitation also includes practicing trusting yourself. A major part of the journey of self-awareness and fulfillment includes trust. I get to continue practicing trusting myself because my activities to explore myself and my range will bring me to new spaces. Those spaces will challenge my trust in myself.

Do I resort to a protection mechanism? Do I cower and throw on my armor?

Or....

Do I connect with what I'm feeling in my body, and where am I feeling it? Do I connect with the thoughts and beliefs rooted in survival, or get present in myself and be an observer of my mind and emotions to extract the messages from within that I have yet to hear?

Men, this is YOUR space to be with yourself, honor and acknowledge yourself, and embrace the value and worth you bring to all experiences in your life.

As I went through each of the lessons I've laid out for you, each lesson supported my appreciation of all that I am. It was like I got a highlight reel of all that I am.

It was my guidelines to steer me to everything I envisioned for myself. To be able to guide and support other Men to their space of self-awareness and fulfillment is the highest level of service and appreciation I can provide to you in person or through the words I've written.

I invite you to be all of who you are. When a Man can practice that, a Man can lay the roadmap for another Man to explore and traverse their circumstances to find, then follow a path that is laid out specifically for them and ONLY them.

Bless you, and thank you for taking this journey. I appreciate you, and the people closest to you appreciate you for going inside and finding yourself.

Here's to you, and cheers to your journey in the Heal.Thy.Man Method.

Bio

Paul R. Newell

paul25newell@gmail.com

Paul is a Soul that is intent on co-creating a heart-full culture of Men by guiding himself and other Men to vibrate authentically in body, mind, and spirit. His intention is at the core of his work in health and well-being, human resources, and facilitation.

Paul is a Men's Health and Well-Being Guide working with *The Mankind Project* and *All Kings*. He facilitates personal development and empowerment courses for men to support them in enhancing emotional intelligence, communication, and connection. He is also the Creator and Host of the *Men Talk About* podcast, designed to guide men in their education, development and inner work to live a life of purpose and fulfillment.

As his Mission of Service, Paul has created *The Heal. Thy.Man Method* to support the education, healing and self-awareness enhancement of Men to transcend systemic conditioning and perceptions to live a life of clarity, purpose, abundance and health.

He also has 20 years of corporate experience in human resources, public speaking, learning and development, and coaching. While he worked in a corporate setting, he fueled his passion for health and wellness by teaching yoga, and delivering health and wellness mini retreats in various communities. He is currently currently a Program Manager for a weekly call for Men of Color to discuss topics that are relevant and resonant to our awareness and our communities.

He is also an experienced Yoga Teacher with 300hr and 500hr Certifications and over ten years experience teaching classes and co-facilitating yoga teacher training. He leverages his experience in both areas to guide others to find their strength and resiliency in their body and their mind.

Connect with Paul on either of his IG accounts (@ newellnessmensguide / @juicedreamsnj), or join him in NeWellness Neighborhood at newellness.club.

www.healthymanmethod.com
www.brothahoodofkings.com